Peter Ho Davies

Peter Ho Davies is the author of the novels *The Fortunes* and *The Welsh Girl*, which was longlisted for the Man Booker Prize, and two short story collections: *The Ugliest House in the World*, winner of the John Llewelyn Rhys and PEN/Macmillan prizes, and *Equal Love*, which was shortlisted for the *Los Angeles Times* Book Prize.

His writing has been widely anthologised, including selections for *Prize Stories: The O. Henry Awards* and *Best American Short Stories*, and in 2003 he was chosen as one of *Granta*'s Best of Young British Novelists. He has also won the PEN/ Malamud Award for Excellence in the Short Story.

Born in Britain to Welsh and Chinese parents, Davies now lives in the US where he teaches Creative Writing at the University of Michigan.

'A funny, tender and unflinchingly honest account of fatherhood, of the ways it can wound you and confound you, but also of its potential for transcendent, transformative joy.'
David Annand, *TLS*

'[It] creates controlled art out of life's messy pain . . . There is nothing superfluous in these pages . . . A novel about the comedy and travails of parenting a "twice exceptional" child that earns its place on the shelf alongside the frank and sometimes acerbic memoirs of Rachel Cusk and Anne Enright.'
Claire Messud, *Harper's*

'His recollections fizz with tell-all voltage'
Anthony Cummins, *Observer*

'Lean and darkly funny, it contains not a shred of mawkishness.'
Stephanie Cross, *Daily Mail*

'Wise, bracingly honest . . . Davies's characters could be anyone, even you . . . this [father] grabs us around the neck instead of by the hand. We are *in it* with him, up to our eyeballs in wonder and coziness, uncertainty and frustration, spousal quibbling and second-guessing. And the all-access pass is exhilarating'
Elisabeth Egan, *New York Times Book Review*

'Davies treats twists of fate with clear-eyed realism, humor, and grace.'
New Yorker

'Astute and heartbreaking but also witty'
People, Book of the Week

'A taut, raw, clever work of autofiction with a real beating heart, this is the audacious tragicomic novel about fatherhood and long-term love we've been missing.'
Claire Vaye Watkins

A Lie Someone Told You About Yourself

PETER HO DAVIES

SCEPTRE

First published in Great Britain in 2021 by Sceptre
An imprint of Hodder & Stoughton
An Hachette UK company

This paperback edition published in 2021

1

A CIP catalogue record for this title is available from the British Library

Paperback ISBN 9780340980293
eBook ISBN 9781444710571

Typeset in Adobe Caslon by Hewer Text UK Ltd, Edinburgh
Printed and bound in Great Britain by Clays Ltd, Elcograf S.p.A.

Hodder & Stoughton Ltd
Carmelite House
50 Victoria Embankment
London EC4Y 0DZ

www.sceptrebooks.co.uk

Without thinking of good or evil, show me your original face before your mother and father were born.—*Zen koan*

In abortion the person who is massacred, physically and morally, is the woman. For any man with a conscience every abortion is a moral ordeal that leaves a mark, but ... every male should bite his tongue three times before speaking about such things.—*Italo Calvino*

There was a chance the baby was normal. There was a chance the baby was not.

Fetus, he told himself. There was a chance the fetus was normal. There was a chance that it was not.

She, he told himself. That was the result of one of the tests on the fetus.

There was a chance that she was normal. There was a chance that she was not.

Jesus.

No one could tell them the exact odds, but there was a small chance the baby was normal. A tiny chance. BB-sized. No bigger than a bean. And there was a large chance she was not. A full-grown, adult-sized chance. Big as a whale, big as a house.

"Stretch marks," his wife said, gazing at the pregnant women across the waiting room like distant mountains. "That's what I used to be afraid of."

Some of the cells in the test were normal.

Some of the cells had too many chromosomes.

The medical term was mosaicism. From mosaic. An image composed from thousands of tiny colored tiles, or pebbles, or pieces of glass. *Tesserae,* his wife recalled from some bygone art history class. Or shells, or grains, or seeds.

The chances of what was wrong with the baby being wrong with the baby had been a million to one.

Before the test.

Except there was still that tiny chance it was wrong.

"A million to one" was a figure of speech, he knew. The condition was so rare there were no reliable statistics. It was so rare the genetic counselor hesitated to put a number on it. *But if you press me.* Fifty or sixty cases worldwide. Ever. So rare that even after a positive test the doctors couldn't be sure the baby had it. But they thought so.

He was a writer now, this father, but he had studied physics once—the science of the unimaginably vast and the unimaginably small, as one of his professors boasted—and still the numbers meant nothing to him. Unimaginable. He didn't like that word—as a writer had a professional dislike of it. Sometimes, he wondered if the baby would grow up to be a scientist. If the baby might make sense of the numbers. What would the baby say in his place, what would the baby decide?

The list of things the baby might have was four pages long. Single-spaced. The list was not numbered. When he cried and stared at it, blurred, it looked like poetry, free verse. Short lines, long lines, run-on lines. He couldn't make any more sense of it than language poetry. He would start to read, and a page in, or less, his mind would drift. Perhaps the baby would be a poet. He felt proud of himself that he wanted the baby to be smarter than him, better than him.

There was a chance the baby would be a poet or a scientist. There was a chance it would die in the womb, live a few hours or days or months in pain. Unimaginable pain.

It was June. The due date was December 7th. "A date which will live in infancy," they'd joked.

Then it was July.

"Chances are, it's not hereditary," the genetic counselor counseled them. She deftly drew the elongated chromosomes upside down on a pad between them. "More likely a spontaneous mutation. A random copying error during meiosis—cell division."

He nodded rapidly. He wanted to tell her he used to be a scientist.

"A freak," he agreed, and her face, radiant with concern, flickered.

"Just bad luck," she said with the infinite care of diagnosis. "Very bad luck."

There was a daycare center down the street. He jogged past it every day. The kids in the little playground. They'd thought it would be convenient, his wife and he. *Lucky,* they'd said.

They'd been used to thinking of themselves as lucky, until a couple of years earlier. They'd just bought their first house, taken a week to unpack, hung the last pictures, shelved the last books, gone away for the weekend. A pipe had burst, a $1.99 plastic tube running into the base of the toilet tank. When they came home, water was running from the light fixture onto the dining table, like a fountain. Water was running down the bulging walls; it was running *behind* the paint like veins. For days they watched dark brown seams spread across the ceiling.

He'd felt like it was God's fault. He'd felt as if it had been hubris to buy a house. It was the worst thing that had ever happened to them in their life together. And yet months later, when they had a much nicer house, they'd kidded each other, *Thank God for insurance.*

They had wanted the house to start a family. They had worried about a child drawing on the bright new walls.

He didn't fault God for the baby. He didn't believe in Him. Couldn't imagine Him. The numbers were too big. They dwarfed God.

They couldn't know—no one could—so they decided, this mother and father. Someone had to and, in the absence of God, it was them. They waited as long as they could. They waited for more tests. They waited with hope, but not hope of good news. The later tests couldn't refute the old ones. The best the new tests could do was confirm the worst. So that is what they found themselves hoping for, as they held hands. The worst.

"Do you ever wish we hadn't done any tests?" he asked her, and she squeezed his hand so tightly he felt the bones must fuse.

The tests were inconclusive.

So they had decided anyway.

And that was all months ago. The baby would have been born by now. They'd have taken the baby home from the hospital by now. The baby's grandparents would have visited by now. The baby would be smiling by now.

Months ago. They were licking their wounds. They were gardening for the first time in their lives, the sunlight heavy on their shoulders and necks. They were starting to tell people they might try again—trying out the idea of trying again, the words ashy on their tongues. They told their friends, the ones who, even though they knew the truth, said encouraging things like "So-and-so had a miscarriage; they tried again."

Once, in bed, in the dark, his wife had whispered to him, "I *wish* we'd had a miscarriage."

It was just a thing people did, he knew. By the kind of chance he was growing numb to, the rhetorical device was known as *meiosis*. Calling one thing something else, something safer. It made his wife furious, but to him it seemed only human, as if the events, the circumstances, so rare, so unheard of, shouldn't have a name. Perhaps in ten years, he thought, it's what we'll say. "We had a miscarriage." It seemed so easy to spare themselves explaining it again, over and over. Perhaps it was what they'd even say to another child, if they had another child. And then he knew it *was* what they'd say, because how could you say what really happened to a child, your own child. If you had another child.

The medical term for miscarriage is *spontaneous abortion*. "You know," his wife said, "the fun, impulsive abortion. The what-the-hey, spur-of-the-moment, fuck-it abortion."

Cars with pro-life bumper stickers were everywhere on the roads that election year. *93% of women regret their abortion. If Mary was Pro-Choice there'd be no Christmas. What part of Thou Shalt Not Kill* DON'T *you understand?* His wife tailed one to a convenience store, followed the driver, a woman, inside. "I wanted to tell her how she made me feel. I was going to, and then I saw her at the register. Know what she was buying? Lotto tickets." They laughed until they cried.

"It's not even the righteousness that gets me," she sighed. "It's the certainty."

"It's not a child, it's a chance," he deadpanned.

The next week he saw one that read *The Number of the Beast? 50 Million Abortions*, and found himself, despite himself, coldly comforted. For once the numbers seemed with him.

"Abortion's been legal my whole life," his wife whispered. "Why do I still feel like a criminal?"

It reminded him of the perennial poll question: *Should abortion be legal under any circumstances, only under certain circumstances, or illegal in all circumstances?* How their circumstances felt anything but certain.

He was a writer now; she was an editor.

"So will you write about it?" she asked. It was his way of making sense. "You can, if you want."

But he didn't know how to make a story of it. The odds were too long. The case too special. "People would only believe it if it was true."

"Nonfiction, then."

He shook his head so slightly it felt like a shiver. "It's too shameful," he whispered. "Not *that*," he called after her. "Too shameful to be this unlucky, I mean."

He stared at the white of the walls. Ashamed, and ashamed of his own shame.

If he ever did write the story, he thought, there was a chance that it would be true, a chance that it would not. A story, at least, could be both.

He rejoined his poker game. Not a game of chance, he knew. But now when he lost a hand, the winner apologized: *Bad beat, man.* The next week, he started playing online. He had always been a good player—good with numbers from his physics days—but he played badly now. Drew to inside straights, chased cards. He figured he was due some luck. But when he told his wife, when she saw the bills, she said, "You think that'd make up for it? You think that'd make it better?" And he quit. But he could tell she thought they were due something too.

There was a chance the baby was normal, he told himself. There was a chance the baby was not.

Even now they didn't know for sure. But they could if they wanted. Somebody did, somebody somewhere in a white coat, in a lab. There had been more tests. Afterward. *Post-*. Finally, the definitive tests could be done. They had agreed to them. *If it helps science,* they said. *If it might help other parents someday. If some good could come out of this.* There were results to these tests and they were conclusive. And they were out there in some file, just waiting to be asked for. "Whenever you want to know, or never," the genetic counselor told them.

Were they those "other" parents now? Was it "someday"?

They talked about trying again, but they didn't. Instead, they talked about the results, whether they wanted them. They couldn't decide about the results. They could decide about the baby, but they couldn't decide about the results. It felt like a cruelty that the results existed. It felt like someone out there with a gun.

They had agreed about everything, but now, sometimes, they disagreed. She wanted the results, and he didn't, just as once and for a year or two, she'd wanted a child and he hadn't. Perhaps she thought he'd come around again.

"Someone knows," she said. "Some doctor, some technician. If they know, I want to know." It was the same argument she'd used when talking about finding out the baby's sex. It had made sense to him then.

"I can't bear it," she said. "The not knowing. How can you bear it?"

He had been a scientist. Could have been one. It was the path not taken. At parties he used to joke that he was a "lapsed" physicist: *It's a bit like being a lapsed Catholic. They still feel guilt; I still feel gravity.* All he remembered of his physics now was the uncertainty principle, and the famous thought experiment about Schrödinger's cat. The cat in a box with a vial of poison; the poison to be released by a random radioactive decay. According to the physics, the decay might or might not have happened, the cat remain both alive and dead, until the physicist looked in the box. Only then, only when observed, would the cat finally be one or the other.

He was thinking, of course, of the baby in the box. Wriggling. Squirming. Heart racing. The gray, grainy baby from the ultrasound that his wife still had somewhere in the house, not exactly hidden away, but put somewhere he wouldn't stumble upon, somewhere he'd have to ask her where it was, as if she were protecting it from him. When he imagined having sex with his wife again, he pictured the milky ghost of his penis, entering her swirling, snowy womb, as if on the monitor at the doctor's office. It looked very cold in there.

He thought of the results. If they got them, the baby would be normal, or the baby would not. Issue settled. But he couldn't do it, couldn't ask for the tests.

All he could think of was the old physics line:

How can you know the fate of Schrödinger's cat without looking in the box?

Throw it in the river. If it floats, the cat's a witch.

He wanted that box to stay shut.

"But why?" his wife implored.

He couldn't tell her.

Why, why, why, like steps, receding.

Not because if the baby was normal, it would make things worse (though it would). But because, even if the baby wasn't, it wouldn't make things better. He didn't *want* to be relieved of this shame, when it was all he could feel, all he was allowed to. All he had left to remember her by.

That was why.

Because the baby was already dead!

There was a chance the baby was normal. There was a chance—tiny and miraculous—that they had killed their baby.

Here was a thing about numbers, he thought for years after. The chance of a flipped coin coming up heads a hundred times is a half times a half times a half one hundred times. Astronomical. But on one flip, the first or the hundredth, the chances of heads are still just fifty-fifty. The coin doesn't care how it's fallen ninety-nine times before. The coin doesn't give a fuck. That's what it is to be random. That's what chance is.

II

Tails

What keeps them together is a child, the chance of another child. They never get the results, can never agree about them except to forget about them. But they start having sex again. Trying again, though it doesn't feel like anything they've ever tried before.

For a while it's the best sex of his life, fervently tender, gravely carnal. He isn't sure if he's pushing something into her, or driving something out.

But she wants it, more than anything, more than ever before; only what she wants, he thinks, isn't him. She wants someone else. She wants a baby more than him.

He wonders what will happen if he can't give her one. He wonders what will happen if he can.

Can they go through all that again? Each month's small bloody despair makes him fear a larger one.

He wonders: When does trying again become trying again and again and again? Become simply trying?

And then, finally, she's late—a day, two, three. She pees on a test stick, sets a timer. While they wait, she reminds him of an early date, one of their first. But what makes her think of it? "I was late then, too! Forty-five minutes or more." When she arrived she was flustered, anxious, expecting him to be mad, but he was just relieved. "I was fine, I had a book. Except I was worried about *you*," he told her simply. Her hair was dark with sweat, he recalls. "That's when I first loved you," she says now. "Because I wasn't *angry?*" "Because you waited."

It's the best sex of his life, her desire so sharp, so zealous, even if it's not for him. Perhaps *because* it's not for him. He can lose himself, abandon himself. The best sex of his life, yet he's relieved when she conceives again, and it's over.

The pregnancy is a vigil. They walk the long hospital corridors as if to the gallows. They brace themselves for test results. They don't talk about what they'll do if it happens again. Perhaps it will be a vindication. Perhaps it will be only what they deserve.

Their copy of *What to Expect When You're Expecting* reappears at her bedside. Whenever he saw her reading it before, he liked to cover his eyes: *Spoiler alert!* Now, he says nothing, expects nothing.

* * *

She never had morning sickness before; now she throws up before every test.

At nights, she clings to her body pillow; he stares at the ceiling fan. In the gloom its three still blades look like the outstretched wings and tail feathers of a giant hovering bird. Eagle. Vulture. Stork, he thinks. The stork of Damocles . . .

A boy this time. The result of one of the tests. They tell no one. They put the ultrasound in an envelope in a drawer in a desk. They don't discuss names. At a dinner party when a friend asks why she's not drinking, his wife says, *If I told you, I'd have to kill you.*

We're taking the Fifth, he explains, making a joke of it. Even the grandparents are on a strictly need-to-know basis. At a stoplight on the way home from a checkup at the start of the third trimester, they look at each other: *Are we now,* she asks, *or have we ever been?* Meaning parents.

Clearly visible in the final ultrasound images: a silvery profile, like the head on a coin.

When the day comes—a scheduled C-section—he sits in a waiting room while they prep her in the OR. It's the summer solstice, the longest day; they've only been here for an hour, and already it feels like forever. He wears what the nurses call a "bunny suit," a clear plastic jumpsuit with a hood. He can see his clothes through the plastic, his bare arms. It reminds him of the Visible Man—that old plastic model kit of the human anatomy, skeleton and organs encased in a transparent shell.

His plaid shirt, open over his T-shirt, looks like lungs. As people pass him, he feels exposed, as if his very skin is see-through. As if he's been flayed. As if he's about to be born himself out of this clear sac. He rustles as he walks when they call him.

Inside, his wife is waiting palely, the sheet tented around her waist like a hoop skirt, blocking her view of the doctors and nurses, their bobbing faces masked, their soothing words disembodied. In scrubs and caps they're indistinguishable from the team at the last procedure, the last time a doctor reached inside her.

Craning, he can just make out her feet in the distance, socked because of the chill. He's reminded of the magic act, sawing a lady in half.

But he's wrong. It's a different trick—*hey, presto!*—a rabbit from a hat.

The baby—face closed tight as a fist, arms and legs churning—begins to turn blue on the delivery table. *Is that right?* the father wonders, and then the nurses, so friendly and solicitous a moment earlier—calling him *Dad*, calling congratulations—elbow him aside, voices stiffening with urgency, and he finds himself pressed up against a cool tile wall, thinking, *Yes, this is it, what we've been bracing for.* Something, almost like relief, seeps through him.

Gowned figures surround the little body—the tiny face, mottled purple as if in rage (*At whom?* the father asks)—and carry it off. He wonders, torn, if he should follow or stay with his wife, calling his name now from behind her sheet. And then it's too late, the baby gone, whisked away. The new video camera in his hand—most expensive of all the new gear—clatters against the wall, and he cradles it instinctively.

He moves back to his wife's side. "What is it?" she begins. "Tell me."

"A boy," one of the nurses says when he can't speak, but that wasn't the question, he knows.

Later, the first glimpse his wife will have of the baby is on the lurid little screen of the camcorder.

Four days in the permanently twilit NICU. Rows of hushed babies in boxes, rectangular transparent boxes (at least you can see what's going on inside them), wrapped in regulation-issue blankets—bet-hedging blue-and-pink striped—the same blankets he'll see for years after wrapped around other babies in emailed birth announcements, always with a stab of recognition. His wife is too weak to visit, so he sits on a stool hunched over the isolette, talking to the baby, willing him to open his eyes, crooning, "Little guy, it's Daddy," whispering it, self-consciously, over the pants and bleats of the monitoring machines.

The seconds drip through the IV lines.

He feels about himself for love, the way he might pat his pockets for his wallet and keys. *Do I love him yet? Is this love?* The nurses say, "You can touch him," and he strokes the baby's toes, his fingers. Gingerly. As if a stranger. Someone has placed a plush beanie toy in the crib—a brindled puppy—he's never seen it before. He wonders if it's some mistake. He thinks of the piles of baby gifts at home, waiting quietly. There's something forlorn about the single toy. He thinks of orphanages, charity. When he holds it out to one of the nurses, eager to give it up, as if it were meant for someone else, she puts it back on the baby. "It calms them to feel some weight." She tells him he can lay his hand on the child, but it seems so heavy, so inert, he thinks he might still the little fluttering chest.

He only gets over it when another nurse—high ponytail, bosomy floral scrubs—tells him to change the baby's diaper. His first resentful instinct: *Isn't that your job?* She stands over him, calling him *Dad, Dad, Dad.* It feels like nagging mockery.

He is starting to get used to it—shuttling between bedsides, his wife's and the baby's, absolving himself with hand sanitizer—and then he goes in and the box is empty, and he feels the tears rearing up in his eyes. "It's okay," the nurse assures him quickly. "They just took him away to do some tests."

He feels suddenly hollow, caved in.

"What tests?"

"An ultrasound. Of his brain, I think."

He knows what an ultrasound is, of course. How many have they had now? This second time around he's come to cherish them, the glimpse of the child, its liquid flicker. But an ultrasound of the baby's *brain?* For an insane second he pictures a baby in there, a baby *inside* a baby, like a tumor. He feels panic, the taste of metal rising in his throat.

"But no one asked us!" he says tightly. "What if we don't want the results?"

She looks at him blankly.

When he tells his wife, she wails, "Why didn't you stop them?"

"They'd already taken him!" But he knows he's failed to protect the boy, the first failure of many, he intuits darkly.

They pace the halls—him pushing his wife's wheel-chair—until the doctors return, casual and smiling. *Oh, the baby is fine. It's nothing. The test was just precautionary.* He looks in their faces—one older, one younger—and glimpses the world outside, a life of deciding on dinner and what to watch, traffic and weather. Incredible to think it still goes on, that anyone can imagine a single moment ahead.

His wife can't stop shaking, doesn't dare hold the baby in her trembling arms. It's a teaching hospital, he knows. He teaches writing at the same university; he understands the model. Sometimes he looks at the work of his students, work gone only somewhat awry, and uses it nonetheless as a salutary warning of worse trouble. *Careful,* he writes in the margin. A teaching moment. This is what he tells himself now: The baby is fine; they were just making sure, following procedure, teaching.

And what has *he* learned? Why, that he loves his son. The thought of losing him, that alarm bell of adrenaline and then the shudder of relief, that's love, he thinks. His heart feels clotted with it, knotted with love, clenched and choking. The abiding fear they've lived with for months, that he'd thought was stalling love, was the thing itself all along. And now it stretches out before him, forever, like a sentence.

Small signs of progress. One visit the cannula is gone. Another the IV removed. The baby's eyes open, tiny and fathomless as two dark distant galaxies. The father wheels his wife in, looks from the baby in the crib to her, pale and lank, in the chair. It's as if they've been in an accident, a crash. But survived.

Only four days after all. Other families, other babies, spend months there. Other babies around him go unvisited. Other babies have a hush about them, a reverence. He looks down the rows of little boxes. He wants his son out of there.

The nurses are like saints. He'll find himself falling, meltingly, in love with every doctor and nurse who cares for the child, but these NICU nurses are special. He can't tell them how grateful he is, promises himself he'll send armfuls of flowers, lavish boxes of candy, though afterward when they're out of there—the baby asleep in his car seat, sitting on the coffee table in their living room—he'll vow never, ever to go back.

He drives home at twenty miles an hour, solemn speed of a funeral cortege.

In their living room, so familiar and yet so strange, as if it's an old photo, faded and curled: their life before. He'd come home once while they were at the hospital, to shower and change, and it had felt as though he'd been gone decades, impossible that the streets were not in ruins, the furniture flocked with dust.

"What have we done?" his wife whispers.

Another thing he'll learn about love: He prides himself on being a good teacher, but he'll never be quite so good again. Some essential love for his students withdrawn, given now where it's due, to his own child. "I guess I really was *in loco parentis*," he'll joke, bouncing the baby, making faces. "Now I'm just a loco parent! Yes, I am!"

And another: He'll keep falling in love—achingly,

tenderly—with anybody and everybody who cares for his child. A series of intense crushes. Daycare staff, preschool teachers, babysitters. Is that how they start, he'll wonder idly, all those dalliances with sitters? As a displacement of this parental love, a spilling over?

And one more: He'll love, almost as fiercely, even the pets—the hamster, the goldfish—those beloveds of the child, simply for staying alive.

The baby has trouble nursing. They feed him formula through a tiny tube taped to the mother's breast and a nipple shield, a ludicrous rubbery contraption that feels like something you'd buy at a joke shop. (*Talk about a letdown*, the mother says wanly.)

The baby has trouble sleeping. They swaddle him as if he were a maniac in a straitjacket and strap him into a swinging chair. The "electric chair," they call it. *Give him the chair!* They play heavy rhythmic sounds at top volume so that THE. WHOLE. HOUSE. SOUNDS. LIKE A. GIANT. THROB. BING. HEART.

At night in the ringing silence, the baby finally, fleetingly asleep, the father lies awake listening, holding his own breath to listen, as if for an intruder, or a mouse in the wall. Even when he can't hear anything, the presence of the new soul in the next room is palpable. He feels himself readied, tensed, even though it's the mother who gets up every time the baby cries. Coming back to bed, in the watery dawn light, she glares at the father, hollow-eyed, furious that he's awake.

Now the baby is nursing.

But now he falls asleep on the breast.

During the days the father straps the baby to his chest and takes him for long walks. It's the only way the baby will nap; the only way the mother will sleep. The father straps on the baby carrier as if it were a pair of bandoleers, mutters hoarse little nonsense ditties over and over under his breath to the rhythm of the forced march. *You are the bay-bee; we are your mom and dad.* He holds the baby's bare legs in his hands as they walk; he kisses the baby's head when it slumps, the drool cooling on his chest, worries his stubble will scratch the tender skin. At crossings, he stands and sways from the hips; sometimes he finds himself—in line at the store, at the whiteboard in class—making the same motion even when he doesn't have the baby. People smile at him on these walks, complete strangers in their gardens, and he nods back. *Can't talk, sleeping baby.* The complicity of parenthood. Except in the student neighborhoods, where the kids avert their eyes as if in disgust.

When he comes home clammy, chafed, shoulders aching, and lays the baby down, it wakes in moments bawling, back spasming, limbs beating.

* * *

The baby was born on the longest day. Now every night feels shorter than the last.

His crying sets off an instinctual panic. Their hands shake; they break out in sweats.

"Perfectly natural," their pediatrician explains. "Like hitting a tuning fork."

Which only reminds him of all the examples of catastrophic resonance in physics books. Shattering wineglasses. Buckling bridges. How are they supposed to help the baby if they're shaking themselves apart?

To the mother the cries feel like blame. A phrase recurs to her—one of her mother's, old-fashioned, but somehow ringingly apt: *a crying shame*. A shame that weeps and shrieks and wails and sobs for all to hear.

And yet a few days later, a stifling summer night, they startle awake to distant crying, only to realize the sound is coming not from inside, but through the open window. They look at each other wide-eyed with confusion—the baby is out!?!—and then it dawns on them: It's *someone else's* baby! Sweet, gleeful relief. It wafts them back to sleep. Ever after, on planes, in hotels, the sounds of other people's babies crying floods him with profane peace.

Things that wake the baby:

A ringing phone.

The doorbell.

The hollow, echoey *bap* of a basketball in the street.

A neighbor's dog.

The shuddery smack of the screen door.

A delivery truck reversing.

The slap of mail through the slot.

A squeaking doorknob.

A groaning floorboard.

An unbalanced load of laundry, thud-thud-thudding.

The pitter-pat of typing.

His grandfather slicing cheese on a plate. *Ting!*

The *smell* of skunk.

A sneeze.

His parents looking at him.

It's their latest version of the uncertainty principle:

The baby in his room with the door closed, the parents outside listening intently in the dark.

Quiet. Or too quiet?

Even asleep in their arms, the long pause between his breaths is enough to set their hearts racing, as if there might never be another.

Dead asleep. Or just dead?

There's only one way to know for sure. But observing the system will change the system.

If he's dead, the mother argues wearily, I'd just as soon find out in the morning.

The father knows, of course, that the uncertainty principle only applies at the quantum level. But how do you weigh an infinitesimal chance against an astronomical outcome? What if there's a catastrophe in the box?

He opens the door anyway, and for once, for a moment, welcomes the baby's cries.

Later in bed he tries to explain Schrödinger, the cat, the box to his wife. Sounds like object permanence, she says. Put a cat in a box and to a baby it's neither dead nor alive, just ceases to be. *Poof!* Isn't that the same? Not really. How isn't it? Go to sleep. I'm *trying!*

Lying there, he knows he's muddling the science somehow, mixing up his physicists (Schrödinger, Heisenberg?), conflating one theory with another.

Maybe the baby will be a scientist, he reminds himself. But that was another baby.

They unplug the phones. They oil the hinges. They blow graphite into the doorknobs.

They see the grandparents off at the airport. (The grandfather has not held the baby once, has gardened the whole visit, expects them to be grateful.)

The cow says, *Moo,* the sheep says, *Baa.* ("The cheese says, *Ting!*" the wife adds under her breath.)

They buy a white noise machine. Now when the father lies awake listening, he imagines he hears voices in the white noise, though he can't quite make out what they're saying. A warning? A threat? He used to joke that he could hear the breast pump talking: "Here it comes, here it comes, here it comes."

At three months, floaty with exhaustion, they sleep train the baby. Set him down and let him cry for one minute— watching the seconds tick away as if they're breaking off something—before comforting him. Set him down and let him cry for two minutes before comforting him. Set him down and let him cry for five minutes before comforting him. They sit on the sofa listening to him cry, fists clenched, ready to strike each other if they dare move before the time is up.

When they read about sleep training in the baby books, it sounded inhuman, but it works. *Not that you ever read the baby books,* the wife reminds him.

The baby is perfect, friends assure them, which only makes them feel imperfect.

He is also a godsend, a gift, a blessing. "What they mean is 'quit complaining,'" the wife says. It's an end to sympathy. A line drawn under something.

Praise God, a cousin writes, but they can't. Not after all they've said about Him. People act like the baby is God's forgiveness, but they still can't forgive Him. Instead, they kneel before the idol of the baby monitor, praying for staticky silence.

An elderly neighbor drops by to tuck a coin, a JFK half-dollar, into the baby's soft fist. An old custom—"silvering the baby"—for luck. Except they don't believe in luck anymore, not good luck anyway; they snatch it away as soon as the neighbor leaves before the baby can swallow it.

Their parents aren't much better. They live far away, but it's more than that. They seem to take everything new parents do as an implied criticism of *their* parenting. *So much has changed,* they say. *We never bothered with car seats; you kids just rolled around in the wayback. Of course, the fashion then was bottle-feeding. Your father smoked like a chimney around you. I used to rub a little whiskey on your gums when you were teething. And you turned out fine, didn't you?*

Relax, his mother-in-law tells his wife.

Don't mollycoddle the boy, his father tells him.

We don't want to interfere, his mother says.

They say they want to help, his wife complains, but they don't want to know how!

He's long used to his parents' disapproval—of grades, career choices, girlfriends. What's new is that now they're dealing with *his* disapproval. He'd always thought them good parents—loving, stable, involved—and still does. It's their anxiety, their defensiveness, their *guilt,* after all these years, that shakes him. Will that be us? he asks his wife, but they both know the answer already.

*   *   *

Changing table, crib mobile, night-light.

Diaper cream, wet wipes, bubble bath.

Onesies, blankies, boppies.

Breast pump, bottle warmer, bouncy seat.

Baby bath, baby gate, baby chair.

All the Tetris pieces to fit—somehow—into their home, their lives, their budget.

The father wanders the aisles of Babies "R" Us, disheveled and stunned as a refugee from some disaster. He stares blankly at the bales of diapers, the pallets of formula, the piled-high bricks of wet wipes. It's the baby-industrial complex, the great American toy chest. Serried ranks of cribs like a cell block. He recalls some statistic that the average child costs its parents $200,000. Presumably, *not* including that $500 jogging stroller, or those night-vision baby monitors, though what's another $500 against $200,000. He's gripped with the sudden realization of how reckless it is to be here—so tired and desperate—with a credit card. He'd give $200,000 right now for a night's sleep.

He emerges with a stair gate, outlet covers, locks for their cabinet doors. To "baby-proof" their home. *Too late,* his wife whispers, *he's already inside the house!*

Once, during those desperate months of trying, she referred to herself as baby-proof. Once she stops breastfeeding, it's what she'll dub her nightly glass of bourbon.

They tape the tiny hand- and footprints taken at birth to the door of what they self-consciously call the nursery. Once, during a nap, the father catches the mother tracing the fine lines with her fingertips.

"They look so stark, so ancient," she murmurs. "Like black-and-white photos from the Depression."

"Marks on a cave wall," he offers.

"Fossilized footprints."

Everything else about the baby is smooth and plump, but here on his soles, in the palms of his hands, he's already seamed and creased with life.

What the father doesn't say, what they really remind him of, is the inky fingerprints of a criminal, a suspect.

The baby learns to lift his head, to roll over, to sit up. He learns depth perception, object permanence—*peekaboo!*

They learn to function without sleep, to do things one-handed, to check their clothes for spit-up. They learn to hold their breath, to control their gag reflex, to lay a towel over his penis when they change him.

He learns to recognizes faces. They learn to make them.

He learns to laugh. They learn to make him.

In years to come they'll learn to sew costumes, build robots, bend balloon animals.

"Did we make a baby?" she asks. "Or is he making us?"

His eyes darken from blue to brown.

Feeding time, play time, naptime, tummy time, story time, bedtime.

Time, time, time.

Days pass like months, months pass like minutes.

They watch entire seasons of TV shows on DVD. *24* is their favorite. That clock thundering like a heartbeat reminding them of just how much can happen in an hour. Jack Bauer's days are so full!

It's like *doing* time, they complain. House arrest. Living under curfew in a dictatorship!

And yet at bath time, bulky diaper and layers peeled away, silky mop of hair plastered to his scalp, the tyrant is so *tiny*. They have to whip his hair up into a frothy meringue, a helmet of spiky foam, just to stop their hearts breaking. (It's "no tears" shampoo—the one product in all the aisles that actually delivers on that promise.)

When they slip hands under his arms to hoist him, his ribs are like twigs. His legs where he pulls them up doughy. But under the hooded towel, his body thrums with life, as warm as if a bulb burns in his chest.

*   *   *

All their newfound entertainment skills—funny faces, funny noises, his white-knuckle marble runs, her baroque pillow forts—are just a response to the crushing tedium, a way to entertain themselves, as much as the baby.

"It's soooooo boring," the mother wails, crossing her eyes, tragic as a teen. "Boredom is good for writers," he reminds her. It's what he tells his students: Remember when you were a kid? Boredom spurred you to daydream, to imagine.

"Bored kids daydream," she tells him now, crossing her eyes. "Bored adults just masturbate."

"Har hardy har," he says. She may have wanted a baby more than him, once. Now, she wants sleep more than either of them.

Super-saucer, shape sorter, stacking rings.

Foam blocks, plastic blocks, wooden blocks.

See 'n Say, Speak & Spell, push 'n' pull.

Like-a-Bike, horsy hopper, Jumperoo.

They will buy anything for a few minutes of peace.

Piles of plastic drift around the living room like the Great Pacific Garbage Patch.

Worse is what the mother calls "Cheerio squalor," the state of filth where Cheerios get everywhere. Under the furniture, in the corners, down the side of seat cushions. "They blink up at me from the air vents!" There are Cheerios in the car, in the coin tray and the cup holders. There are Cheerios mixed in with the loose change in the father's pockets, Cheerios at the bottom of the mother's bag bouncing around with the tampons.

There are Cheerios in their bed!

There are Cheerios in the diaper bag!

And always, somewhere, the terrible tolling tattle of Cheerios in Tupperware—"Bring out your fed!"

Because of the mother's C-section, all those childbirth classes were irrelevant. All those breathing exercises, the coaching, the massage techniques, all that pregnancy tea, all for nothing.

Or not quite.

The father had hated the classes, felt shy around the other couples—didn't want to have to think about other women's breasts and cervixes and perinea—their only bond that they'd all had sex at around the same time. It didn't seem enough to base friendships on. But now here they were—"our village"— the mothers and fathers and babies they'll measure their lives against for weeks and months and years, running into them at Mommy and Me classes, at story time, the toy store, the pediatrician's.

Some of them are fine, he supposes. His wife is close with several of the moms, but the combination of a smart mom, an interesting dad, a bearable baby (non-psycho, non-prodigy) proves elusive. They like one or the other;

maybe two out of three. But really, who wants another baby in their lives?

Back in high school, he tells his wife, he dated a girl whose parents knew his parents from prenatal classes. It had seemed romantic then, destined even; now it just seems random. Especially when everything else in their lives is a careful choice—which diapers, what food, which toys, which sitter. Nothing is left to chance.

That girl, back in high school, had never wanted kids, he recalls suddenly, considered pregnancy, babies *gross*. It had seemed immature to him, but she'd never had them either, from what he can tell via social media.

"Still carrying a torch?" his wife asks.

"For the childless life, maybe." (Which, his wife's face tells him, makes him more of an asshole).

"*All* teenage girls think babies are gross," she explains. "It's not immature, or it's only an immature way of saying they're terrified of getting pregnant." She sighs. "Abortion is shameful, because pregnancy is shameful, because sex is shameful, because periods are shameful.

It almost makes me relieved we had a boy."

They're silent for a moment.

"I hated those classes, too," she tells him. "But it wasn't the other couples. It was all the miracle-of-motherhood, bounty-of-birth doula talk. All the baby-beautiful art on the walls. I hated going because it felt like we were tempting fate."

How far we've come, they tell each other, wondering how far exactly, and if it's far enough, and how much further is left.

Sometimes he has dreams of birth, of the labor they trained for, that she never went through. In his dreams, he moves to the foot of the bed to watch; sometimes he has the video camera with him, sometimes the midwife beckons him. Someone says the baby is crowning, and he cranes forward to look between his wife's legs, and her labia open to reveal a single blue eye staring back at him.

B enchmarks, percentiles, milestones. These are how time passes now.

The baby smiles. The baby makes eye contact. The baby crawls, eats solids, teethes. The baby sleeps though the night. High-five!

Normal, normal, normal, like a pulse.

But also ... he's in the 10th percentile for weight. He arches his spine. They lay him down on his back to sleep, and he arches and rolls over. They lay him down on his back again, and he arches, rolls over. They lay him down on his back again and tiptoe to their own bed, wondering if he'll still be breathing in the morning.

"At least, I can have a drink now," the mother whispers. Another marker.

The baby is one—he walks!—two—he talks!—three—the baby is no longer a baby. He graduates from crib to toddler bed, from pull-ups to potty training, from baby to boy.

At the birthday party, the father jokes, "I always knew he'd turn three—I just wasn't sure I'd live to see it!"

But the boy's preschool teacher has concerns. He's physically wary. Very slow up and down stairs. Skips rather than runs. Behind her back they complain about her, make fun of her overalls. ("She dresses like one of them!") They're grateful for his caution; they still remember the sound of him tumbling downstairs once, the staccato percussion of his head on the wood like a mallet on a toy xylophone. But . . . drip, drip, drip, their anxiety pools. Perhaps we should get him evaluated, they whisper. They don't say tested; they don't say what for.

They take him to the pediatrician, who suggests a specialist.

They take him to a specialist, who suggests physical therapy.

They take him to a physical therapist, who says he's a year to eighteen months behind developmentally. "He's three," the father says. "You're telling me he's *half* his life behind?" It feels like something has been stolen. As if the endless, exhausting months didn't just happen. He wants them back! They drive home slowly, the father's knuckles white on the wheel, the boy chattering away happily behind them.

Once a week: physical therapy. Every day: exercise at home. Whenever he masters something, the boy shouts, "Ta-DA!"

They buy a wobble board, a mini-trampoline; hang a swing in the basement. Every toy in the store—LEGO, Play-Doh, Wii—starts to look like therapy. Catch is therapy. Jigsaws. Hungry fucking Hippos. Nothing is play now; everything is serious.

The father actually enjoys LEGO more than the boy. There's something so satisfying, so neat and orderly about it, the way the bricks go together piece by piece. Why can't IKEA instructions be so clear? Why can't furniture come with *all* the screws? But then he realizes how long it's been since he's written anything, how LEGO may be the most creative thing he's done in months.

He gets cranky when the boy breaks it.

On Sundays, when father and son watch football together— cuddled up on the couch—the boy calls the Baltimore Ravens the "Baltimore Raisins." It makes them giggle.

Afterward, they play catch in the yard, until the boy jams his finger, gets a ball in the face. *It's called catch,* the father snaps. *Not drop!* The sarcasm like a slap.

He thinks of his own father, teaching him stuff—math, riding a bike—the shadow of disappointment that would cross his father's face, when he got something wrong, when he fell or cried. Those hot moments of shame. And now he's inflicting them. Passing them on like genes. And yet, they're so bound up in the love he feels; how to feel one, without inflicting the other?

It's the Age of Dinosaurs.

The boy's particular fascination is with the asteroid that killed them all. He watches a computer animation of the impact—something from a science show—over and over again online, enchanted. One day he draws an asteroid destroying his preschool—*Ka-boom!* The teacher shows it to them with pursed lips; the mother takes wicked pleasure in admiring the bold use of reds and yellows.

The father's theory is that the fascination with dinosaurs, for kids, is a way of thinking about adults—huge figures who can be gentle, or scary. "And who will all be extinct one day," the mother notes.

Also known as the Age of Disney. All those dead or absent parents—Bambi's mother, Nemo's mother, Dumbo's dad.

It's the father who drives the boy to PT each week. An adventure! he calls it. It's not a long journey, but they have to get out of town on the highway, and it reminds the father of road trips they've taken together to his in-laws. All the stuff they point out along the way—firetruck! cow! river! Is that how it starts, he wonders: the prattling parental play-by-play that makes teens roll their eyes? *Over now to Mom and Dad in the booth!* Do our children turn us into our parents?

"Pennsylvania!" he told his son once. "Where the pencils come from."

"Don't tell him that," his wife said. They were driving the long diagonal of the state from football team to football team with only the tunnels—tunnel!—to break the monotony. His son had been demanding another tunnel for the last twenty miles and still his wife said, "Don't tell him that. It's not funny. Do you want kids to laugh at him when he goes to school and says that?" He couldn't imagine the boy going to school. It seemed eons away. Empires could rise and turn to dust.

"Hey," he calls over his shoulder now. "What comes from Pennsylvania?"

But the boy just says, "Tell me!"

"Pencils!" He's hoping for a laugh, but the boy just nods happily like it makes perfect sense. A delayed joke, then, the father thinks, and he smiles picturing the boy years later—in a geography class, maybe, or history—laughing out loud when he finally gets it, thinking back fondly on his dear old dad.

That was the trip, the father thinks, where the changing table in the rest-stop family room had a smattering of pot in its plastic seams.

"Where's Mom?" the boy asks now.

"Home. Fixing dinner. We'll see her soon."

It seems to the father that he prefers it this way. Just the two of them. If the mom were along too, there'd be that constant tension of who was supposed to be tending to the boy, each thinking it was the other, getting mad with each other when they fell down on the job. Once he'd shouted "Cunt!"—not at her but at another driver, not that that made it much better. The boy had said "Cunt" for a week, and even now sometimes they overhear him playing with his scissors, saying proudly, "I'm cunting."

"*Cut*-ting!" the father corrects him. Cutting is good for fine motor skills.

The first time to PT, the boy asked: "Daddy? Where are we going?"

"A really cool gym," he called it. "Just for kids! To exercise. It's going to be some fun."

And in fact this last part is not a lie. The boy loves these sessions, has a blast on the swings and tramps. He's cooperative and attentive with the staff. The father watches, hovering, shouting encouragement—calling the boy "buddy." *Attaboy, buddy!* like any regular dad, like it's sports, though in fact the one time he's signed the boy up for a class at the local Y, he stood by, teeth clenched, tight with worry. Now, he's a PT dad.

Their only previous *attaboy*s were during potty training, as poop coach and poop cheerleader.

PT's really not as bad as all that. He almost forgets the sinking feeling all the way there. It's not so bad. They've nothing to complain about compared to some he sees in the waiting room. When the therapist asks, he's happy to say that, No, the boy isn't fussy about his food, or the clothes he wears, or being hugged. More bullets dodged. But at the end when she's writing down exercises for them to do at home—cross-crawl, bridges, crab walks, Superman, wheelbarrow, dead bug ("More games we can play!" he tells his son)—she adds almost casually they should consider occupational therapy, sensory integration therapy, auditory integration therapy. He might also look into orthotics, if his insurance will pay. She shows the way the boy's ankle ligaments bow outward, and the father nods and says, sure, and how long does she think the boy'll need them, and she says, "Probably for the rest of his life." And he feels himself die a little in that instant—over orthotics!—remembering the boy's first swaying steps, legs akimbo, arms overhead, tiny fists curled around their fingers. Dangling like a puppet.

He looks at his son and smiles brokenheartedly and says, "Okay, buddy, are you ready to go?"

"Roger-roger!" he says in the robot voice of a battle droid.

One day, the father thinks as they drive home, I'll be dead and my son will still be wearing orthotics and thinking of all the lies his father told him.

*   *   *

Besides it's not quite true that the boy's not a fussy eater. All his favorite foods come with cajoling nicknames—*give peas a chance, hav-a-cado, miso tasty.*

His father's specialty is "Mac Daddy"; his mother is "the Celery Queen."

They urge him to *Use the fork, Luke!*

They watch the boy line up and file into kindergarten. It's his first day. They stand on tiptoes to watch him bobbing down the corridor as long as possible. The father imagines he's staring down it into the far future—junior high, high school, college! And then the door closes and they look at each other and wonder what they're supposed to do now.

The mother goes back to work at the university press.

She's always had a horror of being a housewife, a disdain for stereotypical domestic expectations—cooking, cleaning, laundry.

The father gets it, does his bit. It's only fair, they agree.

But secretly he feels she should be grateful. As if he's doing her a favor. As if taking out the trash is an act of love.

And secretly she disdains his efforts. His cooking isn't cooking—his sauces come from a jar. His cleaning isn't cleaning—just tidying.

They're not always great about keeping these secrets.

The one they do keep, from each other and themselves: It's not about housework. It's motherhood hemming her in, the demands of the boy tangled up with the demands of society.

Still, he remembers a time years before, their first Christmas dating in graduate school. He'd had no money to buy her more than a token, but one day when she'd been at the library, he'd cleaned and neatened her cluttered, filthy apartment— folded, hung, filed and straightened, dusted, vacuumed, polished, scoured—until the whole place shone. She'd cried when she'd come in. Their first Christmas with the boy, he was so tiny, propped in her lap surrounded by boxes and wrapping paper, it looked like she'd just gotten him as a gift. The kind she wouldn't necessarily think to buy herself, her faded smile seemed to say, but it's the thought that counts.

The father goes back to work. Not teaching, he's been doing that all along, but writing.

He takes her advice of so long ago, writes about their loss.

A story. Or is it? He's not quite sure himself.

One of the gifts of fiction, he tells students, is the cover it provides. A story can be 1% true and 99% made up, or 99% true and 1% made up, and the reader won't know the difference, the writer doesn't have to declare. It means he can tell the truth and take the Fifth simultaneously.

He likes what he produces, shares it with his wife—the one person who can tell fact from fiction—and she weeps. A *good* sign, he tells himself. He once told students his goal in writing: *I am trying to break your heart.* (Lyric of a Wilco song, he explains, in case they'll think he's cool, in case any of them has heard of Wilco.)

But it's always her heart he wants to break.

It doesn't occur to him that it's already broken.

Instead, he thinks, maybe something good might come of all this. His career is in the doldrums, one slim volume five years ago, a themed collection based on the results of a DNA test, a story set in every region his ancestors hail from. (The ironies do not escape him, nor he them.)

So he sends the new piece out. Maybe it'll be his big break, his *New Yorker* moment. He still feels owed something.

He sends it out, waits, as if for test results. When it's rejected, sends it out again, as if for a second opinion.

And again.

And again.

And finally, a small, fine journal takes it, and he feels ... sick. Defeated. *Is this what it was all for?* As if he's sold his soul for contributor's copies.

Though not *his* soul, he thinks bleakly. And worse than sold it.

"It's not a tragedy," his wife observes. "It's *about* a tragedy." But he's not sure he knows the difference.

"You act like there ought to be some reward for all this," she marvels. "What if it's the opposite?"

He had a novel due, had been working on it for a couple of years when she got pregnant the first time. He has writer friends, several, who finished their books in a mad rush before babies arrived. So many that it had started to feel like a career move, a crafty means of defeating writer's block. But after the abortion, he could never deliver the novel (not least because he sensed the dead metaphor stirring).

"Do you mind," he asks softly. "My writing about it."

He's trying again.

"About us, you mean."

He nods.

"It's your version," she says. "Your side. I didn't take it as the whole story. I assumed that was why it was written like that. That that was what all the breaks were for."

He nods more slowly. (He'd thought he was writing it like LEGO: brick by brick.)

"Of course, I don't know what *he'll* make of it. When he's old enough to read it."

But that future seems so ridiculously distant, a time of flying cars and jet packs, as to be irrelevant.

*   *   *

For a while he encourages her to write about it too. They met in a writing class in college, though she hasn't written for years. And for a while she does. He imagines a collaboration of sorts. But when he asks her weeks later how it's going, she shrugs, says she's stopped. He's sympathetic at first—of course it's hard to make time, of course it's a hard subject to address. He offers to look at it for her, but she keeps shaking her head.

"I deleted it."

"But why?" He can't quite keep the dismay from his voice.

"Oh, I don't know. Why do you care?"

"I thought it might help."

"Well, it didn't. Or it did. I don't know! It helped to delete it. Don't look at me like that."

"Like what?"

"Like *that!* I wrote it. I think I can delete it."

Somewhere the boy is crying.

"I'll go," he says. "I've got it!" she says.

She leaves him alone to think about how he never deletes anything, keeps drafts, fragments, the worst drivel, on his hard drive, in dented file boxes that he lugs from house to house. Even that failed novel. Just in case. Of what, he doesn't know. But the thought of destroying even one page horrifies him. And it's just words, just paper!

And, suddenly, he *does* know. In case of what? *In case I change my mind.*

Later, in the dark, they find each other's hands under the covers. "You'll keep writing about it?" He nods dumbly. Someone has to, but it feels fainthearted.

Someone asks to see photos of the boy, and he realizes the most recent one in his phone is six months old. "We used to take them hourly," he tells his wife, and she makes a face: "Novelty's worn off." Now, they're only dutiful about taking pictures at holidays and birthdays, for the grandparents.

The problem is, in the moment, it's impossible to imagine the boy being any different, or remember him any earlier. The eternal now doesn't need documenting.

An older friend advises: "Write it down before you forget it all." The wife counters: "Maybe we're supposed to forget trauma."

On his first trip away from home after the birth—a conference—the father mooned over pictures of the boy the way he used to pore over ones of his middle school crush. Heartsick and swooning. He bought an extra copy of *In the Night Kitchen* at the airport to read over the phone to a photo. Afterward the hotel bed seemed so vast, it had its own horizon. He stretched out on the crisp white sheets, sank into the down comforter, slept poorly, woke early, the photo smiling silently on the nightstand.

It comes to him he stopped taking pictures around the time they started PT. As for the fancy video camera, it's gathering dust. An obsolete brick. Technology is developing faster than the child.

It's the Age of *Star Wars*. The father had planned to wait, but the other kindergarteners have seen it. He can't risk one of them spilling the beans about who Luke's father is.

They watch it three times in a week, then all the sequels and prequels in quick succession. For months they talk only in quotes.

What an incredible smell you've discovered (on the potty).

I've got a bad feeling about this (before a shot).

Do or do not, there is no try (learning to swim).

Stay on target (peeing standing up).

I love you (at bedtime). *I know.*

The Force is what they have instead of God.

Never tell me the odds (when the father lies awake thinking of tests).

Other parents seem to know each other, to socialize, play tennis or golf. Little circles of them chatting at pickup. "The cool kids," the wife calls them. That high school vibe. They were never the cool kids, either of them. They thought that was all behind them.

"We started late," the mother says, "they're all younger than us."

"A lot of them are locals," the father says. "Grew up here, go back to childhood together."

"Sure. Sure."

"And we're friendly," he says. "Well, you are. We'll get to know them."

But they don't. These friendships with other parents, friendships *based* on parenthood, feel expedient, insincere.

"I sometimes think every other parent is better at it than us," she says. That can't be true, he knows. But what he suspects is true is that none of them ever killed a child. That's how they're better.

The boy's kindergarten teacher has concerns. The mother comes home shaking from pickup. He doesn't play with the other kids. He skips up and down flapping his arms at recess. He can't put his things away at the start of the day or get ready to go home at the end. The other kids are so great at helping him though.

His wife hates the teacher. "I know what she's hinting at. The A-word."

For a moment the father looks stricken. "How could she know?"

"Precisely! What makes her qualified to diagnose autism."

Ah, *that* A-word, he thinks. As if one shame were not enough, now they have two scarlet letters to bear.

They talk with the teacher after class. The father squeezes behind his son's low desk, his legs trapped, as if in stocks. Waiting for the teacher to pelt him.

The boy doesn't participate in class. He doesn't like to color, to draw. He's very polite, mind you. Always says "No thank you."

"Bartleby," the mother says. "I gave birth to Bartleby."

The teacher blinks. "The other kids are great with him though," she says. "They're so accepting at this age, little angels." She beams, beatifically; tiny, bright teeth like a string of pearls.

Is this when he starts hating other kids, the father wonders, because he does. His wife hates the teacher, but he hates the kids. All those happy, healthy, normal fucking kids, running and shouting and playing and climbing, while his boy stands and watches. Stands and watches happily—too pure for envy, too content to feel a lack. How long will that last, the father thinks. How long will I let it? Oh, those loathsome little fuckers.

It shocks him that he loves his own boy so fiercely, hates the others so much.

But, for the sake of the boy, he makes himself set up playdates, welcomes them into his home—the knowit-alls and the why-nots, the finicky and the sugar fiends, the toy snobs and the feral snoops—even as he makes up mean nicknames for them—Ivy the Terrible, Whiny Tim, Will-to-Power, Mimi-me. He can barely bring himself to be civil to their parents when they drop them off, pick them up.

Later, he seethes with resentment when the playdates aren't reciprocated, even though the boy hardly seems to notice.

We should get him tested, the mother and father say to each other. We should, they agree. But they can't. They've been afraid of tests for so long. All his life.

They mark the time now by TV shows. *Wonder Pets!*, *SpongeBob*, *Dora*. These are his phases. These are his pals.

For show-and-tell, the father helps the boy take his hamster to kindergarten. The kids sit in a circle, and the hamster skitters around in its plastic ball. The kids giggle and shriek and call to it, though the father's pretty sure the poor thing is just trying to run away. He hopes the hamster will make the boy more popular. He hopes the other kids won't kill it. "Oh, they're great with animals," the teacher assures him.

When the parents asked the boy what he was going to call the hamster, he wanted to give it his own name until they explained that might be confusing.

"Hamilton?" the mother suggested.

"Chewy!" the father urged.

"Russell," the boy decided. (Too late they'll learn the hamster is a girl.)

* * *

All the tiny shames of parenthood. When your child swears. When your child cries. When your child hits or bites or farts or lies. Not his first word, not quite, but among them, sung out—a happy yodel—from his perch in the grocery cart: *WINE!* Tiniest and worst of all—when your child is weird. When he screams at the hand dryer in a public bathroom. When he avoids eye contact. Yet the child feels no shame— such innocence! And our job, he thinks, the job of parents, is to teach it to them. And he would, gladly, all the tiny shames, if only they might be spared the larger ones.

Summer comes, a break from the worries of school, but also a chasm of time. They fill it with camps—Junior Jedi, Wizarding 101, Dino-might! In every one, the boy will play some version of dodgeball (laser dodge, bludger ball, meteor storm), make soda geysers with Mentos, bring home a sand- wich baggie of slime.

And every day after camp: the town pool, shimmering like an oasis in the distance. The boy's a natural in the water—no balance issues here. Plus, he blends right in with all the other kids skipping on tiptoes across the hot concrete, shivering and shaking off water. All summer he smells of chlorine, grins at his father from under a hooded towel, lips purple from Popsicles, eyes raccoon-ringed from goggles. While he plays in the fountains, the father relaxes, gets in a few laps. The coconut scent of suntan lotion in the water takes him back. But then one day the lifeguards whistle everyone out. There's poop in the pool! The panicky stampede—crying kids, thrashing limbs, flying spray—is like something out of *Jaws*. The father's heart seizes, but the boy is already perched on his towel, hands over his ears to block the whistling. He still insists on his statutory Creamsicle, slurping it mournfully as they watch the lifeguards vacuuming the water. The father is so grossed out, they only go back the day after Labor Day, the last day before the pool is drained, to watch the local dogs dive in.

First smile, first laugh, first words, first steps. First tooth, first haircut, first ice cream, first movie. All of it leading to this: First Grade.

The first time they left him with a sitter, they only made it as far as the coffee shop down the street, only held out for a single jittery hour.

The first time they flew with him—to visit his grandparents—they made sure to pack an extra change of clothes in their carry-on in case he threw up. When he did, it was on the father.

The first time they meet with his first-grade teacher, she has concerns. She's been talking to the kindergarten teacher, it's clear. Words like "skipping" and "flapping" appear again as if in quotes. But it's all innuendo, insinuation. She can't say the word, probably isn't allowed to. (On the poster behind her, *A* is for *Apple*.) The word she uses instead is *last*. To start, to finish, to join in, to get ready.

She speaks to them gently, slowly. "As if we're idiots!" the mother fumes. As if we're the last to know, the father thinks.

The boy loses his first tooth ("Didn't *lothe* it!" he insists, proffering it, shiny with spit, in his palm), lies in ambush for the Tooth Fairy until two a.m. They keep the tooth—"I paid for it," the father says—and each subsequent one, along with a silky lock of his baby hair, because how can you throw them out, these *parts*, these relics? Into a box they go.

All the things they've imagined him growing up to be:

A basketball player, a fireman, a chef.

Allergic, friendless, autistic.

That first lock of hair—a wispy memory of curls. Now, the boy has a buzz cut—they both do—so the straps of his swim goggles won't tear at his scalp, so the boy on his father's shoulders won't yank on his roots, like reins.

At the father's college comes the day to teach Hemingway's "Hills Like White Elephants." The abortion story that never mentions the word abortion. It's a classic, a staple, the textbook example of subtext. He's been dreading it.

Half the class misses it, always. Their reactions when it's explained to them range from a penny-dropping "Ooohh . . ."

to grudging resistance ("Sure, that *could* be what they're talking about, I guess"). He looks around their faces—the faces of those who got it—searching them this time not for critical acumen, but experience, recognition.

But he also resists the story. Its discretion seems perversely coy. Why shouldn't it use the word? (Why, for that matter, should the most famous fiction about abortion be written by a man?) He imagines a revision in which the redacted word is reinserted in every line of dialogue, where the young woman leans across the café table and says, "What are you talking about? Oh, you mean the *abortion*." Where the waiter asks, "Anything to drink ... with your *abortion?*" The bartender winks, "*Abortion*, huh? Tell me about it!" Where the other passengers waiting reasonably for the train stare out at the landscape and chorus, "Why, those hills *do* look just like pregnant bellies!"

Fuck subtext! Screw subtlety! The story normalizes shame. He recalls a similar technique being used in the '80s for stories about AIDS, stories that didn't name the disease. He doesn't teach those stories anymore, and he thinks if he did his students would wonder, *WTF.* He makes a mental note to stop teaching "Hills Like White Elephants," to stop perpetuating the unspeakableness, to replace it with Alice Walker's "The Abortion" or Anne Sexton's "The Abortion," or something, anything, by Grace Paley, said to have started writing stories while recuperating from—you guessed it—her abortion.

He used to tell his writing students: Kill your darlings.

He doesn't anymore.

Or worse: *Murder* your darlings. Both/either are Faulkner's line. Only not only his. Chekhov and Chesterton both had prior claims. Neither had children. Neither did Woolf. Her preferred form: *Kill your little darlings*.

His wife points out that Faulkner actually has a character called "Darl" and *doesn't* kill him. She thinks all this talk of "killing" is writerly posturing.

"It's called editing, darling."

"She said, cuttingly."

Alice Walker has a line in her story—"Having a child is a good experience to have *had*, like graduate school"—which reminds him of Dorothy Parker's quip: "I hate writing. I love having written," which reminds him that Parker had an abortion herself and wrote about it and was mocked for her trouble . . . by Hemingway. As Parker once said of a lover, "Serves me right for putting all my eggs in one bastard."

At pickup, the father stands apart in the schoolyard. Overhead, the aluminum flagpole twangs flatly, whipped by its halyard, a lonely arrhythmic tolling, frantic with desperation on windy days, exhausted and despairing on still ones. He's always surprised by the source, glancing around anxiously as if for someone tapping to get his attention, belatedly looking up. It's the sound of the emptiness before the bell, the doors thrown open, the kids streaming out, the playground filling with noise and motion. How he wishes the boy would come out first. He cranes to look over the crowd, the other parents scooping up kids, looking for his to appear from the shadows of the corridor. The boy's always toward the end, wary of the crush of bodies, the scramble on the stairs, and always the father has a slow moment of dread that he won't appear before the boy steps into the sunlight.

We should get him tested, he thinks. When the only tests he should be taking are the kind you get foil stars for.

Afternoons, after his snack and before his show, the boy continues to do his exercises. His room is filled with brightly colored foam rollers, resistance bands, yoga balls.

At bedtime, when they read to him and the story gets exciting, the boy cries, "Dun-dun-DUN!" (*The sound of an ellipsis,* the father tells one of his classes.)

For months when he was little, it was *Goodnight Moon* over and over, until the father started declaiming it like a poetry reading, tasting every word. He likes to do accents—a drawl for Cowboy Small, a Welsh burr for Thomas the Tank Engine—and impressions: Jimmy Stewart's hemming and hawing ("Wuh, well, goodnight moon"), Elvis's deep twang ("Goodnight moon, uh-huh").

Now they're on to chapter books, each evening a chapter or two, so that the books don't quite make sense to the adults, taking turns to read to him, when they pick them up on alternate nights. It's a little like how their lives feel—mysterious, discontinuous, not quite joined up. Cliffhangers unresolved.

We should get him tested. *Dun-dun-dun!*

All this reading at bedtime, the father thinks, as he browses the children's section of the bookstore. All this reading to aid sleep. He wonders, as a writer, how he should feel about that, the ingrained cultural association of reading with sleep. Isn't it all a little Pavlovian, he muses, watching the heads of his students bob and sink over their books.

But he does it anyway, of course, hunts for those magical tomes that will lull his child. And when he finds one, it sends him to sleep too.

Except maybe it's not the books. It's like a contact high, the mother reckons. Like being tagged in the playground. Sleep is infectious. The boy slumps against him, and he lays back, sets the book aside, feels himself sinking, his body like sand sifting and settling.

For years to come, the father will occasionally yearn for that same warm weight, dense with sleep, draped across his shoulders and chest, recall a voice from somewhere: *It calms them.*

Going on a Bear Hunt. Another old favorite.

Bear up. Bear down. Bear with.

The mother bore the baby, bared her breasts, bears the brunt.

What does the father bear? Apart from the car seat, the diaper bag, the umbrella stroller, the pack-and-play?

At night when the boy wakes with nightmares, it's the father who goes in to him. ("I nursed him," the wife murmurs. "Your turn.") The frame of their bedroom door glows like a portal when the boy turns his light on. The father makes up a story about one of the boy's stuffed toys, a little black bear with a stitched-on muzzle. He can't remember who gave it him; it's not even one of his favorites. The father calls him "Nightbear," explains that the bear's job is to stay awake when the boy's asleep and ensure nothing gets out of his nightmares to hide under the bed or in the closet.

"How?"

"He scares them away."

"He's scarier than a nightmare?"

"He's a nightmare's nightmare!"

"Scarier than . . . zombies?"

"Of course. He scares 'em . . . to life!"

"Scarier than pirates?"

"Aye! He . . . shivers *their* timbers!" He finds a rib to tickle under the covers.

"Nightbear," the boy sighs, when he's caught his breath, holding tight to the toy now that he knows what it's there for. The father eases out of bed, adjusts the shades. Outside it's pitch-black, as if the dark has been painted on the glass.

"Do you have nightmares?" the boy asks sleepily, and the father can only nod.

In the glow of the night-light, the boy thrusts the bear out to him.

"You keep him," the father manages.

But generally the boy sleeps heavily—"like a baby," they can joke now—his body splayed and abandoned as the pile of clothes on the floor of his room. So heavily it's as if gravity is higher in his bed, the father thinks. So heavily, it's as if—like a black hole—no consciousness can escape its pull. Overhead pale stars fade on the ceiling, plastic planets tremble on their threads.

Except once during sex they were startled by the boy's rustling wakefulness—"It's . . . *ALIVE!*" they whisper-screamed to each other—and now some part of them always listens for him when they touch.

It's the Age of *Harry Potter*. The child flicking spells—*Expelliarmus, Expecto Patronum*—off a chopstick like drops of water, the mother and father casting fake ones back and forth in a duel.

Fettuccini alfredo!

Pasta fagioli!

Hakuna Matata!

Carmina Burana!

Ginkgo biloba!

In Vino Veritas! (They clink glasses.)

In Loco Parentis!

Is that a spell, she asks, or a curse?

At college, his class roster reads like a list of baby names circa 2000. Three Dans, two Matts, an Ellie, an Amy, an Emma. Laura, Lara, Lauren. A Michelle and a Rachel, who both go by Shelly. Jake and Jacob, Ryan and Bryan. A Kate and a Cat. So many choices, so many of them the same.

The first time she was pregnant with the girl, they joked about names. (Brie? Cheesy!) The second time they didn't pick until the boy was born.

At the boy's school, the talk is of observations and accommodations, of sequencing and processing, of IEPs and

504 plans. There were teacher conferences; now there's a learning team. When the talk turns to executive function, the father isn't sure if it refers to the boy or the school.

Through the window the flag flails silently against a cement sky.

Emails arrive daily from the PTO asking for volunteers. To chaperone field trips, to serve as lunch monitors, recess monitors, after-school tutors, assistant coaches. All of them well meaning, civic-minded, the right thing to do. And yet it infuriates him to be asked. Aren't I doing enough, he wants to say. Isn't it hard enough without doing your job too? Don't I have enough to feel guilty about?

The latest physical therapist, at least, is pleased with the boy's progress—his muscle tone, his core stability, his bilateral coordination. "Way to cross that midline!" She's so good with him—patient and smart, but also genuinely warm—another caregiver it's impossible not to fall in love with. The father feels her praise is for both of them, for all the work he and the boy do together at home. He blushes when she calls, "Good boy!" Of course, she's too good for an affair, like a saint or a nun, and like the other PTs built with the kind of firm solidity he finds more admirable than attractive (though he occasionally fantasizes about the boy's swim teacher at the Y, also wonderful with him, and great-looking in her red lifeguard suit, a tattoo twined around one calf). And then it comes to him that he's attracted to them all because he thinks the boy would approve, that they'd make good mothers. And it feels like a double betrayal.

At Halloween, the father wears a wolf head. He is the Big Dad Wolf. The mother has a moose hat complete with antlers: Mommie Deerest. These will be their costumes every year for a decade, while the boy will be Nemo, an astronaut, a Jedi, Harry Potter, Robin Hood, Mr. Spock.

The father didn't grow up trick-or-treating. He used to find Halloween unsettling, with its focus on monsters and evil. There seemed something unwholesome about exposing kids to that, to death. But now he gets it, that it's a celebration not of fear, but of its opposite: trust. He trails the boy around the neighborhood, holding his breath as his son negotiates the crowds, his costume, unfamiliar porch steps, but also watching in wonder as total strangers open their doors to him with enthusiasm and kindness. He tells the boy, when he takes his hand, that the cold makes his eyes water.

It's better than Easter, at least, when all the other little shits outrace the boy for eggs and he comes home in tears.

Sometimes they vie for the title of "sparent," the non-essential parent. *I'm the sparent. No,* I'm *the sparent.* But is it self-deprecation or selfishness? he wonders.

Once she wails, You'd both be better off without me! And he clutches her as if to stop her leaving there and then, tells her he can't imagine life without her.

It's true—he can't imagine being the father without the mother.

It's true, but also a rebuke. Don't you *dare* imagine life without me, he wants to tell her, without him.

And yet without the boy . . . could he imagine his life without her then? Shit, he can barely *remember* their life together before the boy. It's impossible to imagine them without him. Without him, what would they have?

What about that time we forgot it was Halloween? she asks after the boy has counted his candy, gone to bed. How *could* we? This was another town, another state, early in their marriage, long before the boy. Kids had come to the door, and they'd been caught empty-handed. Horrified, they'd ransacked the kitchen for granola bars, cooking chocolate. When even those were gone, they'd switched off every light in the house, huddled in the dark, as children knocked on the door, listening to the silence, and then walked on. They had held each other, stifling laughter, slid to the floor in an embrace, fumbled each other's clothes off.

The wife costume. The husband costume.

Now look at us. Mom jeans. Dad bod.

Trick-or-treat? She smiles sadly.

They should get him tested. Instead they're testing their marriage.

He drives babysitters home at night, sits in his car to watch them safely enter their apartments, feeling like a stalker himself, gripping the wheel, fighting the urge to follow them into their childless lives. It's not *them* he wants—in person he feels more tender toward them than aroused—but their freedom. He'd hit *that*. He resents the money he pays them, only because it feels like they're already richer than him.

The boy's favorite show, the Sunday evening ritual after his bath, is *America's Funniest Home Videos*, which he calls "America's" and demands as if it were a human right. "They wouldn't show it if anyone *really* got hurt," the mother reminds the boy every week. She means it as both comfort and warning; he regards her as a killjoy. The father's tailbone throbs in sympathy watching all the pratfalls, but he tells himself maybe it'll make the boy less physically cautious. When they all go to a friend's wedding, the boy is delighted, and then bitterly disappointed. He expected someone to fall over on the dance floor, destroy the cake at least. Breaking the glass is a poor substitute. He yanks on his little tie in

71

frustration. "What's the point of weddings if something doesn't go wrong!?!"

The mother and father look at each other, straight-faced.

At home LEGOs speckle the carpet like confetti.

Early in their relationship, they had all the usual uncertainties. "Just" friends or friends with benefits? Dating? Exclusive? Boyfriend and girlfriend or partners, a couple?

Even when they got married, he realizes, it hadn't seemed quite settled, life changing, irreversible. They'd done it at a courthouse near her mother's place—a small, quick affair, before moving across the country. After a one-night honeymoon, they went on as before, already living together. They hadn't bothered to register—their friends were even poorer than them. Cash was fine, they told family, less stuff to pack. They didn't even have a new toaster to show for it. He'd looked at the ring on his finger and thought, "Huh, now I'm a guy who wears jewelry." Did they *feel* married? they asked each other. They didn't *not* feel married. And she didn't much like his efforts to "perform" marriage, to play-act it, hated him calling her "wifey," even in jest, called him "hub" with a cringe, hated everything that smacked of sitcom marriage.

There was an awful, awkward breakfast at the B&B where they spent their wedding night when the other guests learned they'd just gotten married and burst into applause. And they blushed—bride *and* groom! Marriage was mortifying.

Even his proposal was casual, impromptu. They were on an outing—a beautiful day in the park, a picnic, wine—everything so right it felt like inspiration. "What do you think? Should we get married?" And she shrugged and smiled and said, "Sure. Why not?" As if it were a dare! And he liked that she didn't need a ring, tied a grass stem around her finger, with a little emerald knot. "I'll cherish it forever," she said. "You better," he said.

Love was a joke, shared.

Even when they got wedding rings later, they could never think of inscriptions, could never quite settle on a word, a phrase, to engrave in perpetuity, not even "forever" for forever.

What did they see in each other? he sometimes wonders. What did they have in common? Their lack of commitment!

So maybe it hadn't been serious until they had the boy.

No, he amends sternly, until the first time she got pregnant.

It's the Age of Tricks—magic kits, yo-yos, juggling sets. The boy gets them all for Christmas. They seem more like dirty tricks to the father. Coins refuse to vanish. Balls refuse to appear. Rings refuse to separate.

It's torture watching him shuffle.

Is this your card? Is *this* your card? IS THIS YOUR *CARD?*

But he loves practical jokes, gag gifts—whoopee cushions, snakes in cans, rubber spiders, and plastic puke. They fall for them—aargh! eww!—over and over to his undiminished delight. *Just like America's!* he crows, the joke on them. Sometimes it's okay to be tricked.

Every few weeks that spring, there's another birthday party at another fun venue. The whole class is invited.

House of Bounce, with its stink of socks and vinyl.

Sip and Slide, the caffeinated jungle gym.

Golf of Space, the indoor, glow-in-the-dark putt-putt course, with the black-light mural of that astronaut hitting a drive on the moon. *Fallin' Water*, with its slides like giant plumbing, its pool the temperature of warm piss. *The Hands-on Experience*—aka "The Germatorium . . . Sponsored by Purell." Oh, the places you'll go!

The *best* thing about birthday parties is that they can drop him off for two hours. It's almost the only time they have sex anymore, the only time they're alone in the house.

Sneaking around like teenagers when Mom and Dad are out, they tell each other.

Sex, yet another in that long line of secrets they keep from him. Santa, the Easter Bunny, the Tooth Fairy. All that parental sneaking. All those lengths to hide our roles. What are we ashamed of? he wonders.

One of these days, not so very far off, there'll be sex ed in school, she reminds him.

Oh god, he groans, the *talk*.

That's on you.

Why me?

He's a boy, isn't he?

Implied: the notion that she'd have had the talk with the girl.

The birds and bees, he says.

And then there'll only be one secret left.

The D and E, she whispers.

The boy comes home spacy from cake and soda, too busy inventorying his goody bag—sucker, check! stickers, novelty eraser, bouncy ball, check!—to notice his parents' moony languor.

Hosting *his* birthday parties meanwhile is as stressful, as exhausting and ritualized as a royal wedding.

For his latest, he begged for a label maker, this boy they're so afraid of labeling. "A what?" "He *lurves* the one at school, apparently." So they got him one (though they gave it to him before the party), and he happily punched out labels all morning on the tiny keyboard—MY ROOM, MY CAKE, MY PRESENTS—stuck them up everywhere. They laughed uneasily, until one of the other moms pointed out, "So cute! You guys are writers, yeah?"

Later there'll be a neat label on his office door: BEWARE OF THE DAD!

For the mother's last birthday, the father bought her a pair of noise-canceling headphones and she almost wept with gratitude. She wears them so much he's jealous, says she looks like a Mouseketeer. *What?* Oh, never mind!

When the boy flaps his arms or bounces around, the therapist calls it "stimming," short for self-stimulation. "He's seeking vestibular input," she explains. "Think of it as overflow movement," she says, and the father finally gets it. The boy's body *is* overflowing, with energy, with joy, with excitement, even as he himself often feels his own heart overflowing with sadness, the emotion ready to spill in him like a brimming cup that he has to hold steady. A cup of blood, as he pictures it, something precious and staining, dreadful and embarrassing to spill.

He watches his son, snapping his wrists as if shaking off water, high-stepping up and down, humming to himself, and envies the purity of his happiness, his solitary self-sufficiency.

Sex is relaxing, restoring, rejuvenating . . . until the moment she thinks the condom might have broken. *Get off me!* The bright fear in her eyes.

A friend once told him, "I used to think we got married for sex. Now I think we have sex to stay married, just so we don't bite each other's heads off."

It reminds him of that other wry couplet: Some people get married to have kids; some people have kids to stay married. He wonders which they are. If either.

A brief history of their relationship in birth control:
Pulling out (the first time).
Condoms.
Female condoms (once).
Diaphragm (UTIs).
IUD (cramps).
The pill (mood changes).
Condoms.
Nothing.
Breastfeeding.
Condoms.
We could try anal?
You could get a vasectomy.

* * *

He's considered an affair. He has grounds: fourteen years of faithful marriage (*double itchy*, as the wife herself joked at their anniversary). And in return? The only occasional toleration of his desire.

He buys her lingerie; she wears it as if it's fancy dress. What he finds sexy, she finds eye-rollingly ironic.

Most mornings he settles for stubbing out his erection against her ass. *The crack of dawn*, he jokes. *Fuck Dawn*, she murmurs rolling away.

He'd taken to masturbating during her pregnancy (*re*taken, naturally, it was like riding a bicycle), and kept it up, so to speak, ever since. Masturbation had come a long way since he was a boy, he found. All thanks to the internet, of course, but what struck him most was not the sheer volume and variety of images available—though they *were* astounding; less stimulating than boggling—but the realization of how many people out there were looking at this stuff. Masturbation had always seemed so lonely to him as a teenager, part of its shame being how aberrant it was. (Dimly he senses this is somehow the point of the internet: to spread shame, but so broadly, so thinly, like a light coat of varnish, that we hardly notice it anymore, until we all just glow faintly with it.) Now, judging from what he could see on his computer, the masturbators far outnumbered the couples, and were probably getting more action. Frankly, it has gotten to the point that he's come to prefer it—quicker, more efficient, less cumbersome than intercourse—something for which he feels only an obscure sense of infidelity. Less risky, too.

Three, four, five times a week, like some horny high schooler. His self-stimming. Sometimes he fears he's addicted, not to the porn, not even to the act itself, but to the shame it provokes. As if it's shame he's coaxing from himself, his body.

Still, every so often he weighs a real affair, albeit idly. The problem, more practical than moral, is that he can't quite imagine sex with another woman. Marriage has rendered the act so mundanely intimate. It's the slurp and slap of bodies coming together and apart. It's the furtive postcoital stroke to disguise the rubbing off of bodily fluids on one another. It's his wife's fingers discreetly rolling the linty pills of toilet paper out of his ass hair, or the shivery quake when her cunt farts.

("Trumps," they call these.) It's her yelp of pain when he pins her hair under his elbows, or the little *ouf* (less of passion than pressure) she releases when he lowers his weight onto her. These are the things that have undermined their sex life, but they're also what keep him bound to her. Who else would put up with such indignities, who else could he share them with? Ass lint has no place in an affair!

Marriage, he notes ruefully, is a terrible preparation for infidelity.

But if intimacy is filled with shame; shame—shared and secret—is also intimacy. Shared shame seems to him as close as most of us ever come to forgiveness.

Just once, home alone, mother and baby at story time somewhere, he glimpses a pair of lace panties in her drawer, wraps his fist in the watery silk. He remembers this pair, kissing her through them, drawing them off with his teeth. Even remembers the hot flush of embarrassment choosing them in the store, as if he were choosing them for himself, which in a sense he was.

Now they're a relic. Imagining her in them as ridiculous as slipping them on himself. Which he does. The fit snug, tightening as he grows hard until they clasp him like her hand.

He's suddenly furious at her, ashamed and hoping to shame her, but his orgasm, when it comes, feels dismally faithful.

And once when he complained she was never in the mood, she told him, "Thanks! Like I don't have enough to feel guilty about. No really, fuck you, you fucking fuck!"

A long-singed silence. Then he whispered, "How about now?" and she burst into laughter. "I mean that's the most action I've had in one sentence." "Stop it, I'm going to pee myself!" "Was it good for you, too?"

* * *

All this talk of affairs. A compensation, he knows. Sure, he'd like more sex, but he doesn't doubt her love. What he doubts is his manhood, not in bed, but on the playground, at play-dates, at pickup, when he's often the only man and the women, the mothers, eye him warily and then, once he's established as a dad, ignore him. "Invisible Manhood," he calls it.

Why did the invisible man turn down the job offer?
He couldn't see himself doing it.

There's another father at school with a whole line of them. The only other man in the playground.

What did the buffalo say when he dropped his boy off at school?
Bison!

If you don't tell Dad jokes, you risk becoming one is this guy's philosophy.

A preemptive strike, an ironic acquiescence. The father used to think he was witty, himself, used to love making his wife laugh, used to get jealous if she laughed out loud at something she was reading. He dimly recalls some idea of Freud's about a woman's laughter—the spontaneous, unbidden physicality of it—and orgasm.

Dad jokes, though, aren't for laughs, but groans.

A furniture store keeps calling me. All I wanted was one night stand.

*   *   *

That year all the dads are dressed like kids in comic-book tees. How come all the boys want to grow up to be heroes, his wife asks, but none of the dads want to grow up? The Age of Superheroes is just another excuse to not act your age.

Maybe, he thinks, because so many origin stories begin with a father's death. Batman, Superman, Spider-Man (the boy's favorite): it's how they become men.

And how many of them ever become fathers? Well, there's Reed Richards, Mister Fantastic of the Fantastic Four. Not *Something*-Man, but *Mister*. Just like a dad. He's even graying at the temples. And this dad's superpower? He's stretchy, bendy, elastic. Like Gumby, or Silly Putty, or Stretch Armstrong. All arms to reach and hands to catch. Able to pack healthy lunches *while* emptying a loaded dishwasher! That's who's on the father's shirt.

It is the Age of Speed.

All the other kids have those folding metal scooters. The boy shows no interest. They buy him one anyway.

All the other kids ride skateboards. All the other kids ride bikes.

The boy is still on training wheels.

We should *really* get him tested, they tell each other.

Instead the father hires a guy who teaches bike riding to the disabled.

They meet once a week in a school parking lot. The father watches furtively from his car.

And one day the boy just gets it—*I'm DOING it!*

And shakily, snakily, then surely and smoothly, he is.

A triumph for him; a failure for the father.

They should get him tested. But it's starting to feel as if getting him tested is a test they're flunking.

Meanwhile, the occupational therapist teaches him how to tie his laces, how to button his shirt, how to hold a pencil.

God, the mother says, what is even the point of us?

"Scarier than a vampire?"

"He drives them batty?"

"Scarier than a werewolf?"

"He turns werewolves into *were* wolves!"

"Scarier than Frankenstein?"

"He drives him nuts . . . *and* makes him bolt!"

"Scarier than a mummy?"

The father looks at his wife.

"He makes mummies cry Uncle!"

The mother blames herself for everything, though occasionally she extends the blame to the father, too. They should have done this; they should not have done that. In the back of both their minds, he knows, it's all the same guilt. He feels it too, but not like her, not like a mother. And eventually he resents it. She *is* guilty, he thinks, guilty of feeling guilty. *That's* her fault. It makes her despairing. It makes her say things over a glass of wine like "We should never have done this." It makes her say things like "We ruined our lives" and "It's never going to get any better," after another. It is as if she thinks the boy is their punishment.

She blames herself for everything but the wine. "I have you for that."

His own vice is sugar, which he substitutes for sleep. Cookies and candy are his uppers; he hides a stash from the boy. His wife calls his favorite brand of caramel corn "crack corn."

One day the boy toe-walks all the way home from school. I *begged* him not to, the mother wails, but when he asked me why not, I didn't know what to say. He was *so* happy! She wept all the way home.

The father calls a shrink for her, schedules a meeting. An act of love he wonders, or blame?

I thought we were supposed to be getting *him* tested? she grumbles. But she goes.

Goes, and says it helps.

Yeah? *Yeah.* And . . .? *And we'll see.*

He gets it, wants to respect her privacy. But it makes him feel alone.

Well, I'm relieved. *I bet you are.*

H e's been thinking about volunteering. As an escort. At a clinic.

He's been thinking about a man's part in abortion. What he can do, what he can say.

It's a good thing to do, he tells his wife. A good time to do it. His college classes have ended for the year, the boy is still in school for another two months.

You're supposed to be writing, researching, she reminds him.

But maybe this is his research. Maybe it'll become writing.

Maybe it's his therapy, she suggests.

Maybe it's his test, he thinks.

They never went to a clinic. Their procedure was at a hospital. What's sometimes called a therapeutic abortion, as

87

opposed to an elective one. They never had to pass any protesters.

He makes a call, schedules a meeting.

We had an abortion, he thinks he might say.

But can *we* have an abortion? he wonders. Or is the male use of the first-person plural in this context as suspect as saying, "*We're* pregnant"? Something his wife always scorned. Yet if the phrase "we have a child" is fine, couldn't "we had an abortion" also be viable?

Of course, he knows the unease with that use of "we" is more complicated. If it's a woman's right to choose, after all, what role does that leave for the man? Agree or disagree, it's her choice. (Though wasn't she *his* choice? he thinks. And he hers?)

I want to help, is what he says instead. I just want to help: itself a plea.

Typically male, he understands. This desire to fix something, to protect someone. He knows his chivalric instinct is as rusty, as clanking and ungainly, as a knight's armor. But aren't other men just as backward, as atavistic? And aren't many of those men on the other side of this fight? To speak to them, to combat them, maybe his instincts—retrograde as they are—might be some use. He hopes so.

"A virtuous abortion" is what the escort coordinator—a fireplug with a steel-gray perm—calls it. Her name is Barb.

They meet at a coffee shop. She asks him why he wants to be an escort and he tells her, "My wife had an abortion" and the circumstances.

A virtuous abortion. She says it matter-of-factly but it still shocks him, hearing this shame called virtuous. She's trying to remind him that his story isn't the same as others', that theirs aren't the same as his. That everyone has their own abortion. And yet, he feels judged, slighted even. As if their abortion were somehow lesser. He knows what Barb means, of course. They weren't some teenagers who'd forgotten to use a condom. They weren't underage, or high, or poor, or Black. Or even unmarried. They didn't fit any of the usual categories of blame or bigotry. No, they were white and middle class and married and trying to have a baby. They had an abortion within the bonds of holy matrimony.

He isn't sure how virtuous that makes it.

He's still smarting a little at the end of the interview when Barb asks if he has any questions, and he realizes he wants to ask *her* if she's had an abortion. And then he realizes he doesn't need to.

It reminds him of going for the procedure with his wife. They had known somehow, just *known*, that all these women—the nurses, the doctor, even the receptionist—had gone through it too. Without anyone saying. Something about the quality of their sympathy. It had come to them like a balm that they weren't alone.

(One in four, he tells his wife later. The chances of a woman having an abortion. He's read it on the clinic website. One in four. Not a coin flip, of course. But also not a roll of the dice. In fact, the exact chance of flipping a coin twice and calling it right—two heads, say—both times. I'm no expert, she advises, but you should probably try not to say "two heads" when you talk about abortion.)

That evening at dinner he watches the boy carefully separate the foods on his plate. He doesn't like them to touch.

Everyone has their own abortion, the father reminds himself, just like everyone's kid is different.

He asks the boy about his day. He's typically vague. It's as if he walks out of school and forgets everything that happened inside by the time he gets home.

In return, the boy asks about *his* day—his wife looks up at him—and he ... lies. Because, of course, you can't tell a child. What he feels, he realizes bleakly, his instinctive response, is to protect the child from even the word abortion, the very idea.

But when Barb calls him the next day, invites him to the clinic to shadow her, he sets the phone down with relief. As if he's passed something.

"Let's try a shift a week for a month," she says, "see how you do."

*　　*　　*

It is the Time of Screens. Screen time: a drug dispensed in careful doses. It makes them irritable if the boy has too much. It's Angry *Birds,* not angry words, he mutters.

But it allows them to eat at restaurants in peace, his little head bowed over a device as if saying grace. Another tiny shame, pocket-sized.

They fill their phones with educational games with names like *Math-a-Magician* and *Gramma-Ray.*

They bargain earnestly. Make him read a book first, as if *Captain Underpants* were good for him.

The father stays awake into the small hours, leveling up.

Someday soon they know he'll start begging for a phone of his own; someday slightly less soon they'll give in. "He'll never be bored," the father says, a respite from their need to entertain him, but also a loss. In his memory, childhood feels less like innocence than boredom, long blank stretches punctuated by vivid moments. "He'll have the attention span of a goldfish," the mother says. So maybe he will be bored, the father thinks, if our distraction devices are always that little bit slower than the flicker of our attention. "He'll never be *alone,*" she concedes. But this, too, seems alien to the father, an only child, loneliness the constant companion of his childhood.

So much of his parenting, his teaching, those instincts, are based on his recollections of being a child, a student. What does it mean that his son's youth will be nothing like his?

*   *   *

His first day escorting, Barb meets him at the same café, tells him what to expect at the clinic. "What to expect when you don't want to be expecting."

He spills sugar on the table, brushes it away, slops his coffee.

"Should be a quiet day," she says. "Most days there are a handful of protesters, a couple dozen on the weekends. Their big shindig every year is called the Jericho March—there are at least a hundred then. But that's not until Easter. They march around the building, tooting everything from tubas to kazoos, hoping the walls will come a-tumbling down. Lot of nuns." Barb calls it "The March of the Penguins."

She calls days when the crowd is thick "heavy"; days when it's thin "light." She smirks at his blushes.

She checks the weather every morning. It helps predict the turnout. Good weather—more protesters. Filthy weather—fewer. Today's forecast: "Cloudy with a chance of assholes."

By chance, the boy has a kazoo. By chance, they own the DVD of *Cloudy with a Chance of Meatballs*. By chance, penguins are the boy's favorite at the zoo.

"Excuse the bad jokes," she says. "Old habit." She was an EMT for twenty years before she retired. "Whatever gets you through, am I right?"

It's a purple state but a college town, so the protests are

mostly peaceful, she goes on, "if you can call that racket peaceful." At least there's no "speed-bumping" or "hood-surfing," terms that sound like so much skater slang to him, but which she explains refer to protesters lying down in front of cars or spread-eagling themselves across them, respectively.

"What about"—he lowers his voice—"guns?"

She shakes her head.

"Never felt the need of one.

"Seriously," she adds, "we're careful, of course. But their chief weapon is shame, shame and intimidation, intimidation and shame ... Their *two* weapons are shame and intimidation ... and lies ... their THREE weapons are shame, intimidation, and lies—"

"And an almost fanatical devotion to the Pope!" he chimes in.

"Huh!" She grins. "*No one* expects the Spanish Inquisition sketch! You'll do."

And it dawns on him that *this* was the test, and not of his sense of humor exactly.

After a recent session his wife noted: I was always brought up to think of therapy as a little, you know, shameful.

And now?

Now I think everything's relative.

* * *

They call it a "prayerful presence." *Do you have children?* they ask him.

They describe themselves as "prayer warriors."

Do you *have children?*

Women they turn away they call "saves," which makes him think of soccer.

Barb is orienting him. They're both wearing pink neon vests, emblazoned with the clinic logo.

She calls them "antis." He heard it from her mouth as "aunties" at first.

They call her "Nazi," "butcher," "baby killer."

They ask him, "*Do you have* children?"

Barb's been an escort for four years, ever since she retired. "Better than being a greeter at Walmart!" Though in her nylon vest she could pass for one.

They offer to pray for him. "Thanks," he tells them distractedly, adds sheepishly, "That's okay. I'm fine."

He knows he's not supposed to engage them. It's policy.

"But that's awfully boring," Barb tells him with a wink.

"You get to know them," she says, "the regulars." She points them out. They're clustered on the sidewalk between a scrubby grass verge and the mouth of the driveway, where a painted white stripe marks the property line. "That's Mary with the rosary, Mitch with the candle. He used to kneel, but he had a hip replacement last year." She gives him a wave—*Mitch!*—and the man brandishes his Bible. "Helps to know their names if you can. To defuse things. Sometimes you overhear them; sometimes they volunteer them. Sometimes I make them up—I had a Norm and a Cliff for a while. Helps to recognize them, any new faces stand out. Regulars have regular behavior. Newcomers are wild cards."

I'm a newcomer, he thinks.

Do you have kids?

"Helps if they know your name, too, or think they do."

Barb is not Barb's name.

"It's my stage name." She taps her name tag. "After Barbara Bush. Makes me smile when they're cussing me out." He sees the resemblance suddenly in her tight, rosy cheeks. "Who'd you wanna be? George? Donald? Dick?" She cackles.

Do *you* have kids?

When they ask him his name—"So we can pray for you"—he blurts, "Sam."

"My father's name," he confesses to Barb. He doesn't tell her they'd considered calling a girl Samantha.

We're praying for you, Sam, they chorus.

"*I* have kids," Barb murmurs almost wistfully. "Two boys. Grown and gone. Don't hear from them one season to the next." She shrugs. "I tell myself, 'If they take you for granted, it means you did something right.'"

It's the last place he expected to find a mother figure.

*   *   *

At the clinic she hands him an umbrella, even though the sky is clear, even though there's an awning for them to stand under. "For clients," she says. It's a big golf number with a long silver ferrule, which makes it feel a bit like a lance or a spear. He leans on it, trying to feel dapper, trying *not* to feel like a doorman. Still, he likes the idea of holding an umbrella for a woman. It feels courtly, chivalrous. But, when the first women arrive, Barb has him open the umbrella to shield them from the antis. It makes him feel like the Penguin in *Batman*, maybe Gene Kelly, though he resists the urge to twirl it.

"It's spitting," Barb explains, and she doesn't mean the weather.

There's nothing "virtuous" about any abortion to the antis, he knows. Even those "certain circumstances" of the poll question—the life of the mother, say—are off the table now. Barb's line—after a protester brought her own daughter in to the clinic a few years back—is that the only exceptions the antis believe in are *rape, incest,* and *me* (and not even those first two sometimes!). She means it as an example of hypocrisy, but he clings to it—the uncertainty of principle—as a tiny glimmer of hope.

He picks the boy up from school after his shift and takes him to Dairy Queen—just reopened for the season—even though it's turned into a brisk spring day, sky ribboned with cloud. They're the only ones there. The boy looks up from his Blizzard and says slyly, "This place is deserted!"

"DQ?" the mother asks him, looking at the father. "What did you do to deserve that?"

For ten minutes the worst that could happen was brain freeze.

Later that night she tells him, "I'm sure it's a good thing to do; I'm just not sure it's a good thing for you to do."

He wonders what that's supposed to mean.

He wonders if she's been talking about him in therapy.

His next shift Barb points out other faces in the crowd. Ted in his trench coat. Martin with the long beard of a prophet. Keith, a skinny Black man with a diamante cross on his chest ("You bear it well, Keith!" Barb calls). Bald Dale peering myopically over a lurid sandwich board. Joan dressed for church with her hat, gloves, and patent leather handbag filled with flyers. Eileen with her empty umbrella stroller, trying to look tragic, but coming off like an absent-minded grandma. Several are old enough to remember when abortion was illegal.

Some are too shy to cause much trouble. Just bearing witness—"silent but deadly," Barb calls them. Then, there's your chanters, your hymn singers, your screamers. In between are your "sidewalk counselors." Less shouty, but still a nuisance. They won't physically obstruct, but they do like to approach clients, talk to them. Polite at first. Lots of *ma'am*-ing. Jeans and ties. They want to ingratiate themselves, convert people. They hate the screamers almost as much as us.

Barb has nicknames for many of them. Ted is "the Flash"; Martin is "Gandalf"; Dale is "Kilroy."

They call her: Nazi, butcher, baby killer.

Stan-the-stache is a Vietnam veteran, wears a fatigue jacket, a cap with an MIA patch. His hair is a close-cropped gray, and when he shouts his scalp flushes red beneath it. "I always wonder if someone called *him* 'Baby killer!' when he came home," Barb murmurs. "How'd he like it?"

Barb is a vet herself—Army Nurse Corps, Gulf War One.

"Sometimes, I end up protecting *them*," she tells him. "From boyfriends usually, or husbands, come to support their girlfriends and wives. Men! I get between them and the protesters, break up any eye contact, distract them with small talk about the weather, sports, whatever works. Remember the antis want a fight, but they want *our* side to start it, so *they* can call the cops.

"Once," she tells him, "a man came back outside for a smoke. Asked me if we had cameras. Asked if I'd switch them off for a minute."

"What did you tell him?"

"Can't do it, sweetie. All that'll happen is you'll get hauled off and your lady will be alone. That's not why you came here today. Am I right?"

He nods heavily, as he assumes the boyfriend or husband nodded.

"They call me names," Barb laments. "But do they ever thank me?"

She expects him to look out for these men now, he knows, but he rarely does more than exchange a nod with them. "You might as well just grunt," she notes. If one of the husbands or boyfriends went for an anti, he thinks, he'd as likely join in as break it up. He feels a dark, vaulting joy at the thought.

In the lulls when no one is coming or going from the clinic, the antis pull out phones like everyone else. "What's an anti's favorite app?" Barb asks. He shakes his head. "Blocky Road!"

Barb has a friend, a sympathizer, who lives nearby and makes a point of walking her retriever by the clinic each morning, letting it shit on the verge where the protesters gather. "It's the little things," she says, with a grin.

The boy's current favorite movies are about a golden who plays basketball, football, soccer. (The father remembers when the only games dogs were good at were poker and pool.) "Watch with me," the boy asks, but he has another shift.

("Barb, Barb, Barb," his wife says. "She's got her hooks in you, all right. How old is this Barb?"

She knows; he tells her again. What she's getting at is a different infidelity. The same one he wonders about when he asks if her therapist is a man. There are affairs, it turns out, and affairs. Affairs of the heart, affairs of the conscience, affairs of the soul.)

And then there are the clients, the women. By his third week, he starts to know them, too. By the set of their mouths, the stiffness of their shoulders, their eyes.

Not all of whom are there for an abortion, Barb reminds him. Some for contraception, some for breast exams, pap smears. "So don't go getting all gooey. They might only have a yeast infection or a UTI." The clinic only conducts procedures on certain days of the week, shifting the schedule periodically to try to throw the antis off.

Some are there for medical abortions: the abortion pill (two to be exact; one taken at the clinic; one later at home).

And then there are the women—further along—who are there for surgical abortions. The ones with no makeup or jewelry; who come with a friend or partner to drive them home; who look hungry, because they've been fasting for eight hours.

"Though many still wear their wedding rings," Barb notes. "More than come with their husbands, actually. Of course, some are afraid to tell their partners," she explains, "but some just want to spare them the guilt, to protect them. Remember *that* next time you're feeling all manly heroic."

She teaches him to give the women space, to never approach a car in the parking lot, to walk a step or two behind as a shield. But instinctively, he finds himself hurrying ahead at the last moment to open the door for them.

"Really?" Barb asks afterward. "I guess chivalry isn't dead." As if chivalry were a particularly tenacious roach.

Some of the women run, some of them cry, some of them shout back.

"What if your baby cures cancer?" the antis call.

"What if *I* do!" a young woman, a student by the look of her, yells back.

"Your baby might be Jesus!" they implore.

"My baby might be a girl," another shouts back.

"Your baby might be Dr. King," they tell Black women.

"My baby might be Malcolm!"

Your baby might be a scientist or a poet, he thinks. Your baby might be rich and famous, a leader, a hero. A gentleman, a scholar, or an acrobat. Or poor, or sick, or a woman seeking an abortion.

All the coin flips. All the *what if*s. Like the litany of prompts he uses in writing class. Heads and tales.

He admires the women who shout back, but Barb shakes her head, tells him sotto voce, "They win if they get you to call it a baby." She admires the ones who wear headphones.

"Some of them cry. Some of them laugh after," Barb tells him. "They're relieved, or they're guilty. They want to talk about it, or they don't. And it's all normal. Some of them just need to hear that."

He nods. He understands the need to be normal.

Some of them smoke, which startles him at first.

Some of them thank him, which makes him blush.

"I just walk them to and from their cars."

"It's maybe a little further than that," Barb says. "They've so many strangers calling them names, judging them. Not just here—online, on TV, out there. It means something to have another stranger say it's okay."

The kindness of strangers.

He doubts it goes far enough, surveying the out-of-state plates in the parking lot.

Some of the women have driven for hours to get here. Six, seven, eight hours. Sometimes through the night. Barb's found them sleeping in their cars when she opens. They can't afford a hotel, can't afford to miss two days of work. All those miles for this! Nothing but right-wing talk shows, Christian radio, and classical music for company.

He thinks of those long cross-country drives with his wife when they were younger, moving from job to job. How lonely those drives would be for one, how bleak, without the talk, the companionable silences. Sometimes his wife would sing along under her breath to the music. He never heard her sing otherwise, not even in the shower. He wasn't sure she was aware of it. He'd be very quiet, still in his seat, not wanting to make her self-conscious by drawing attention to it, not wanting her to mind him beside her, loving her silently, as if he were glimpsing her alone.

He wonders if these women sing to the radio. Hopes so for their sakes.

(In the car with the boy, meanwhile, all they've listened to for a week is "Who Let the Dogs Out." When he mentions it to Barb, she grins. It's one of the songs the clinic plays to drown out protesters when their chants gets too loud.)

Just once one of the women sees his wedding ring, tells him fervently how lucky his wife is to have him. He shakes his head and she thinks he's being modest. But it's not that. It's been so long since he's thought of either of them as lucky. And yet compared to most of these women, he knows they are.

*　　*　　*

That afternoon, Barb asks him to stay late so she can show him how to close up—to turn on the cameras, to set the alarms. First, she hands him a bucket and broom, sends him out to the sidewalk, to where the antis have chalked prayers and slogans.

Abortion kills twice, he reads, *a baby and a mother's conscience—Mother Teresa.*

"No bigger expert on motherhood than a nun," Barb says, scrubbing away. "I mean, c'mon, it's right there in the name."

The boy's mother once chalked a hopscotch court on their drive to improve his balance. The ghostly outline of boxes still visible even after rain.

Because of the shift he can't pick the boy up from school that day. His wife goes instead.

That night they fight in scorched whispers.

"I have a job," she reminds him.

"You act like it's a hobby—" he begins.

"And you act like it happened to you! You were just there. It happened to me!"

It happened to us, he wants to say. It happened to you, yes, of course, but it also happened to me, because I love you. Wants to say, but can't because for a moment it isn't true.

Instead he reminds her that he is the morning person. He wakes the boy, makes his breakfast, packs his lunch, walks him to school. She may have gotten up nights for a year; he's staring down a decade of six a.m. starts. His schedule is more flexible, so he's often the afternoon person, too. Picks the boy up, gets him a snack, arranges playdates. Sometimes he feels more like a waiter, a valet, a secretary, or a chauffeur than a father.

"Oh, poor you," she hisses, "you barely have time to be a knight in shining armor."

All the doors he's held for women down the years. A tiny gallantry still appreciated by many. Now the gesture makes him think of how he'd told her it was her choice, told her he'd support whatever she wanted. How saying those things was like holding a door. *After you.* So fucking polite. It's a woman's right—no question—but a part of him thinks that lets men off the hook, spares them something. It *was* her choice. But if you hold a door open, aren't you ushering someone through it? *This way, please . . .*

She never liked the term "choice" anyway. Says it smacks of capitalism, the market. Choose a phone, choose an outfit. Like shopping. It's *nothing* like shopping! It's not a choice, if there's no other choice.

Books have started to show up on her nightstand, books with "anxiety" and "trauma" and "healing" and "mindfulness" in their subtitles. Recommendations from her therapist. He's shy of them, as if they were her diary, afraid to touch them, afraid of what he might find. They've had so little privacy, the two of them, since the boy was born.

At school it's Art Fair (or "Fart Air," as the boy insists on calling it, correcting them dutifully, as if it's a contractual obligation of first grade). They sit through performances— massed recorders, xylophones—and wander the echoing halls hunting for his art, their disquiet spiraling as if it's him they've lost. When they finally find it—one muddy abstract, the paper stiff and buckled with paint—they stand before it in silence, the three of them.

"What is it?" the father asks, and the boy shrugs. "Art."

When they ask the teacher at their next conference what else he's been making, she sighs, produces a folder of collages. "It's all he ever wants to do. The other kids call him 'The Rock,' because he's always with paper and scissors. They love wordplay," she simpers. While she's putting the folder away, the father leans close to the mother, whispers: *"I'm cunting!"* And she has to clutch her mouth to stop laughing.

Flexible schedule or not, it's not always easy balancing his teaching and parenting. "But," as a colleague has joked, "a kid is a good excuse. You can cry off evening events—readings, lecturers, dinners—cut out of meetings early for pickup, plead recitals and soccer games." Art Fairs. "A good excuse *if* you're a man," another colleague, notes acidly. "Men get to have it both ways." She means he also gets to duck bath time, bedtime, sometimes to go to functions.

For a couple of years, he kept a third option—telling his wife he had to work, his colleagues he had to parent—in reserve, folded up tightly, in case of emergency.

But now he wonders: Is volunteering an excuse? And if so, for what?

On a break at the clinic, Barb introduces him around. The doctor offers brisk thanks, a handshake as firm and dry as a diagnosis, the anesthetist, a serene welcome, as if she expects him to fall asleep before the end of her sentence. When he tries to engage them—thank them in turn for their work, their bravery—they blink. "It's a legal medical procedure," the doctor tells him, "nothing more, nothing less." She's not wearing a mask, but she might as well be. (Later Barb will tell him that she does often don disguises to come to work— glasses, hats, wigs—never wears the same outfit in that she wears out.)

He talks longer with one of the nurses, Jenna. She's similarly down-to-earth if more forthright. "People get too bent out of shape over a few cells. We're not talking life-and-death here. We're talking *potential* life-and-death, something women deal with every month." One of her jobs is to conduct the ultrasounds that women are obliged by state law to view before they get an abortion. "They don't actually have to look—I tell them they can close their eyes or turn away—but *I* have to do it anyway." She sighs at the injustice, the existential pointlessness of her job. The staticky images as dreary to her as black-and-white TV. People still *ooh* and *aah* over the techno-marvel of ultrasound. To her it's just a cheap magic trick. "Hey, presto! The lady vanishes! And what's this? A fetus! Ta-da! As if the woman didn't even exist."

He knows from physics, from the uncertainty principle, Schrödinger's cat, that we can't observe anything without changing it (any more than as a writer he can't retell something without changing it). He asks how many women change their minds when they see the images. "None," Jenna says.

Everyone knows another word for cat is pussy, he thinks.

And everyone knows pussy is another word for clit is another word for cunt is another word for snatch is another word for twat is another word for gash.

But not everyone knows another word is box.

In the box in the thought experiment, before it's opened, there's a chance the cat is alive, there's a chance the cat is dead. But theoretically it's neither alive nor dead *before* it's observed. That's what's inside these women, he reminds himself—not a baby, not a fetus—just a chance. Another word for another word for another word. And the word for that, he knows, is meiosis.

Jenna it turns out is also an alias. "Last name Tulls," she tells him with a slow smirk, waiting for the penny to drop.

Found on the Planned Parenthood website as part of his research: a cute cat video, part of an explainer on female sexual anatomy.

https://www.plannedparenthood.org/learn/health -and-well-ness/sexual-and-reproductive-anatomy/what-are-parts-female -sexual-anatomy

You can't make this up, he thinks.

His son's new best friend is Siri.

So play with him, his wife snaps. He misses you.

The boy likes to take photos with their phones. An acceptable hobby, they decide. Maybe he'll be a photographer. At night the father looks through them—feet, clouds, suddenly himself—the back of his head while driving, his hand on a fork, a slice of the mother stooped over the sink. Is this how he sees them?

He shows the boy photos he's taken of him, centered in the frame. The boy flicks through them at dizzying speed—kindergartner, toddler, baby—as if his life were a flipbook. All the way back to the hospital, and fast-forward again.

Nazi. Butcher. Baby killer. Barb calls it "stoning."

When his wife asked him about facing the protesters for the first time, he joked: "Worst workshop ever!"

Comes a bright spring Saturday, daffodils budding on the verge, the biggest crowd he's seen so far, spittle shining in the sunlight.

He marvels at how a painted white line can hold them at bay, like magic. "That's no line," Barb tells him darkly. "That's a *fault* line, the crack in America! You can't have politics, democracy, if one side thinks the other side are baby killers." He wonders what she thinks of the other side, what she calls them to herself ("antis" seems so mild by comparison). "Sexists? Fanatics?" She shakes her head. He's hoping for one of her salty quips—*Motherfuckers*, maybe— to lift his mood. Finally, she says: "You want to force a woman to do something with her vagina she doesn't want to do? You're a rapist."

He glances over, but her face is stiff, scanning the crowd. Nazi. Butcher. Baby killer. "Names, names, names," she chants under her breath. He's getting warm in his nylon vest. Barb, too, by the look of her. She flaps the collar of her blouse, and he catches a glimpse of a gold star at her throat. Sweat prickles his nape, his hairline. Nazi. Butcher. Baby killer. "How do you stand it?" he asks her, raising his voice over the din. "How do you stay so calm?" It's mid-afternoon now, their third hour. His legs are trembling a little, his jaw hurts from clenching, his shirt clings. "For them," she says simply, meaning the women. If their blood pressure gets too high, she's told him, the procedure has to be delayed.

Hence the wisecracks, the nicknames.

Nazi! Butcher! Baby killer! At first he thought they only meant Barb.

At first he thought his rage was for her, on her behalf. Protective. Sheltering.

Baby killer. He feels something loosening in himself. It's so hot. He feels his pulse throbbing in his fists. *Yes,* he thinks. *Yes I am! And what makes you think I stop with babies?*

He's staring at Martin, mouth writhing in his beard, picturing blood on his teeth, blood from his nose, blood flecking the gray. Picturing him crumpled on the sidewalk, curled up in—*yes!*—the fetal position. Picturing Dale with his grisly sign, recoiling ashen-faced from the gore.

Suddenly, he feels Barb's arm on his. His throat is raw.

"Easy there, fella. Easy!"

There were no protesters at the hospital where his wife had her abortion. All they had to worry about there was running into pregnant women, new mothers.

"It still didn't *feel* very virtuous," he explains to Barb later over a beer. ("You look like you could use one," she said at the end of the shift.)

"I'm sorry," she says. "No offense."

"Virtuous abortions," she acknowledges, "for fetal abnormalities from rubella, from thalidomide, were important in getting the conversation about abortion going in the sixties. I just wish the conversation could have moved on a little since."

Virtue, he knows all too well from the invective outside the clinic, is something denied women getting abortions. They're whores and harlots, terms almost as old-fashioned as virtue. Or, come to that, chivalry.

"'Virtuous' abortions are tragic," Barb is saying. "Regretted. Sympathetic. I get it." She looks at him softly, and he sees that she does. "But they're also rare—one in a hundred. And if those are the only stories that get told, then abortion in general seems tragic, when most women who've had them say they don't regret it. Oh, they might regret the *circumstances* that require one, plus all the bullshit around getting one, but mostly they're relieved." She sighs. "Asking for sympathy is just an other way of asking for permission."

He nods, he knows this.

One of the women he walked back to her car asked him the time. She had three other kids, needed to be home to fix dinner. They bonded over mac and cheese, Velveeta over Kraft.

The chance of a woman having an abortion already being a mother: 60 percent.

He asked another, shyly, if she had any regrets and she nodded.

"About five hundred of them," she said, rubbing her fingers together. What she paid today. "Cheaper than another, mind you."

The chance of a woman getting an abortion being under the federal poverty line: 50 percent.

"What a gentleman," she said when he opened her car door for her.

He'd watched these baby killers come and go all day.

Theirs might not be virtuous abortions, he thinks now, but they all seemed less guilty than him. Too busy for shame, too poor in time and money. As if shame were a luxury. For them it's not a choice, with all the handwringing that entails, so much as a necessity. And it seems to him that many of them are making a virtue out of that necessity. He envies them that.

"Necessity," Barb agrees. "It's a mother, all right."

He envies them their relief, too. Envies it, and worse. Some are downright cheerful, giddy, to have it over with, as if it were a tooth extraction. He catches himself wishing they were more circumspect, more somber. More ashamed, he thinks, burning with shame himself for thinking it.

But why shouldn't they be relieved? This isn't the trauma—this is the trauma averted. Next to an unwanted conception, an unwanted birth, what's an abortion? A dread lifted. Freedom to get on with life. As Barb put it once, "Abortion is life changing, sure, but also life *not* changing. That's the point. That's why people do it. It's something that happens, but also something that doesn't happen."

Perhaps that's why it's so hard to write about, even to talk about, a climax that doesn't change anything. Perhaps that's why the story of regret is so persistent (though a part of him suspects *every* story is a story of regret; that we tell them to redeem ourselves).

He tells Barb at the bar he doesn't think he can come back, and she nods, relieved herself, he sees, that she doesn't have to tell him not to. He can still feel it, the adrenaline tremor of murderous rage. Like nothing he's felt before, except it reminds him of the way the baby's crying summoned something similarly instinctive in him.

"This wasn't even that bad today," Barb says gently. "They're actually a lot worse when both escorts are women. Fucking sexists!" She makes a wide-eyed *Who da thunk it?* face.

"It's just the way they *weaponize* regret," he rails. "And then we deny it."

"You know," she says, "I didn't mean to suggest before you two shouldn't have regrets. How you feel is how you feel, obviously. I'm just saying everyone has regrets. You know who has regrets? Parents is who."

He raises his glass. "Damned if you do, damned if you don't."

* * *

Later, he will understand that he's not been at the clinic to do good, or even to gather material, so much as to find absolution. But he's been looking in the wrong place. The doctors and nurses, Barb, can't absolve him for something they don't consider a sin. For them the Coca-Cola and saltines they offer women after the procedure are just that. He wants them to be some kind of communion.

In fact, it's *them*, he realizes with a dull pang, the antis, who are the only ones who can absolve him, forgive him. Because they believe he's a sinner, and secretly he agrees. That's why he hates them, really—because they won't.

Later still, he will understand that all these feelings—his, his wife's—just won't fit between the lines, between the sides. In the political box. He doesn't want to argue about those feelings, to defend them or justify them, he just wants to be left alone to feel them.

At home that night, he scoops the boy up in his arms, inhales his warm sweet scent, pulls his wife in to the clinch.

"You okay?" she asks later when he tells her he's done at the clinic.

They're on their knees picking up marbles.

"Yeah," he sighs. "What about you?"

She nods slowly, as if surprised herself.

The marbles go into a Tupperware. *Plink, plink,* like prayers.

"I just wanted to help," he whispers.

"I know."

He rolls the last marble, a blue cat's-eye, back and forth between finger and thumb.

"But what if you can't?" she asks. "I know you want to protect women. Fine. But who do you think you're protecting them from? Who do you picture? What if men *are* the problem? What if abortion at root is an undoing of the power of men? Can a man help with that?"

He opens his mouth, closes it.

Didn't he say the selfsame thing about the US in the Middle East? Not that help wasn't needed, just that America—so tarnished, so compromised by the invasion and all that followed—couldn't offer it. Too much a part of the problem to be the solution.

She takes his hand and squeezes.

"What if you can't help, but I told you it was okay? That I wouldn't love you less? That *I* need your help? Here."

And he nods, swallows. "I'd still like to donate."

"Sure. Yes. Of course!"

"It's not like *I* don't have regrets," she says, taking his hand. "About a million of them. What do you think I talk about in therapy? But I wouldn't have done anything differently."

He sighs. "I think I need a drink."

"I don't," she says, reading him. "But I'll keep you company. And yes, we talk about that, too. You know what she reminded me? That the first drink I took, the first time we were pregnant, was after we got the final diagnosis, after we'd decided."

He pours two glasses of red, raises one.

"Regrets."

They touch rims silently.

"Except," she whispers leaning close as if for a kiss, "it's not really regret, you know. It's grief."

III

Heads, Twice

They get the boy tested. At long last. They sit in another waiting room, waiting. A special doctor they tell the boy, assure him there will be no shots. "Promise?" The doctor takes his hand, leads him away. I've got a bad feeling about this, the father thinks. The judgment of the world. He feels it turning inexorably from himself to the boy, wishes he could shield him from it, fears he's destined, like all parents, to only be the lens that focuses it.

Another waiting room, but always the same lonely activity cube in the corner. He can't recall a kid spinning its gears or flipping its alphabet tiles in anything but the most desultory way. On top there's always a bead maze. Sometimes, its scribble looks like a model of his brain. Today the tangle of multicolored wires makes him think of a bomb he needs to defuse.

Tick–tick–tick.

He's seized by the sudden need to get out of there.

But by then the receptionist is calling them back. The tests are done, done, done.

The boy is what's known as "twice exceptional," the doctor says. They look at him blankly. "Gifted," he says, "but also challenged." They look at him blankly.

"Autistic?" the mother whispers.

The doctor smiles softly, and they start to exhale.

"Somewhere on the spectrum, probably," he says. "Spectrum-y, spectrum-ish—best not to get too hung up on labels. Atypical, yes, but very high functioning."

The father thinks of a prism, the light refracted into its constituent wavelengths. The boy has a rainbow night-light that works on the same principle. "It's a very broad spectrum," the doctor adds. "It's hard to say for sure."

The father nods (some wavelengths are invisible, he recalls from his physics); the mother cries jaggedly; the doctor looks embarrassed.

"All I want is an answer," she sobs. "All I want is to know. Is that too much? Either/or. Heads or tails. But what you're telling me is *both*. Both!" she spits. "It's like some fucking good news/bad news joke.

"No!" she snaps at the father when he puts a hand on hers. "I just want it to *stop*."

The doctor discreetly assures them of a full write-up to follow.

The father feels dazed. His heart had lifted at that word, "exceptional." Now he feels tricked, sucker-punched. The boy's exceptional, except . . .

He flashes on the line of Fitzgerald's. "The test of a first-rate intelligence is the ability to hold two opposed ideas in the mind at the same time." Another test. But not of intelligence (that just seems like so much flattery). To him it seems suddenly like a test of humanity.

While they compose themselves for the boy to reappear, the father says quietly, "I'd probably be on that spectrum if they'd ever tested me as a kid." She looks at him—he braces as if for a blow—takes his hand tightly in hers.

And then the boy is there, beaming around a lollipop. He likes this doctor—zero shots!—enjoyed the games. They walk out hand in hand in hand, swinging the boy between them.

"Can we come again?" he asks.

"No!" the father tells him, and his face falls.

Lately, when refused, the boy's taken to sighing heavily, adding a dutiful "Well, please?" Not as if it really is a "magic" word, but as if they think it is. As if it's some irksome game he's outgrown like Simon Says.

But this time he stays silent.

The mother reads up on it, but the father has never cared for the bogus debate about vaccines. To him it just seems a way of finding something or someone, anything and anyone, to blame. He understands the desire, but he already has people to blame. Himself. God. Not that they can ever be brought to account. Vaccines, drug companies, doctors, will just have to get in line.

Twice exceptional ... half functional, the father catches himself thinking in the weeks that follow as he watches the boy put his clothes on backward, shrug on his backpack before his coat. It's the impatience talking. He wills himself to breathe, to think of the boy—his capacity for joy, his gentleness—as a child half full.

He'll still seethe, mostly inwardly he hopes, at the show-offs and prodigies, the gifted and the precocious. But he will also study the parents of more severely challenged kids as they wait together in waiting rooms, study them with admiration and sympathy and a shame-filled aversion indistinguishable from relief. They're saints and martyrs, and he wants nothing to do with them.

They decide to change schools. The father lets the mother tell the teacher on the boy's last day.

There are other options, smaller schools, private schools. Not cheap—the father will have to teach summer session— but not required to administer standardized tests either. ("No tests!" They high-five the boy.)

"Oh, yes, a lot of our kids are 2e," one principal tells them. "We love them."

"Project based," "child centered," she says, but it's the word "love" that they'll gladly, gratefully pay for.

2e being how the diagnosis is abbreviated. Almost as if it wasn't exceptional at all.

2e or not 2e, the father can't help thinking. The next question.

That summer is their museum period: the era of natural history, the epoch of ancient civilizations, the eon of planetaria. *It is the Age of Aquariums,* the mother sings, *the Age of Aquariums . . .*

Normal, normal, normal. They do all the normal things— hot dogs at the ballpark, cotton candy on the boardwalk, glow sticks on the Fourth. Look at us, he thinks, just like everyone else. Fake it till you make it.

That August: a family vacation. San Fran, Monterey, LA. And for one shimmeringly hot day, Disneyland, mecca of childhood. His own parents never brought him; he never quite forgave them.

They get there early to do *everything* (even if the most heart-pounding adrenaline rush turns out to be finding a bathroom after the boy drinks a Goofy Glacier). By the evening, his wife is crying with tiredness on Main Street, fireworks glittering in her tears. She's been complaining about Disney's California Adventure—the fake Fisherman's Wharf, the faux Santa Monica Pier, the fiberglass redwoods and plywood Sierras. *We're in* real *California! Why's everybody here?* Happiest place on earth, he reminds her sternly, the boy slumped asleep on his shoulder. But what he means is: the normalest.

The report the doctor promised arrived before the trip. The envelope is still waiting when they return. The wife tears it open like a scab.

He's fine, she says afterward. The same, unchanged, himself. *His* normal.

She is laughing and crying.

We're the ones who are fucked up. What were we so afraid of?

The worst, he thinks. That's all.

S econd grade is a second chance. Another flip of the coin. But for once, luck seems to be with them. The place they liked best is expanding, moving to a new building, taking new kids. The teacher loves the boy, the boy loves the teacher, the parents love the school.

It won't necessarily last, they know, but they cherish it all the more for that. You only know luck by its opposite.

Behind this new school, across a parking lot, behind a line of dwarf conifers, and beyond another parking lot is a low, blank building. Windowless, unmarked, facing away. It could be the back of a box store, some generic office building. It happens to be the clinic he volunteered at.

They don't share a street, which is why he didn't realize before, but he confirms it on Google Maps.

You couldn't make that up, he thinks. You couldn't put that in fiction. How could you? It's so contrived. No one would accept it. But there it is. Life is a terrible fucking writer.

He spots Barb at pickup one afternoon doing her rounds. After a moment she waves back. "Well, look who it is!" He walks over, holding the boy's hand tight as if they were crossing a busy street. "Hello, cutie. What's your name?"

The boy tells her shyly, but soon grows bored with the adult pleasantries, asks if he can go play. The father is relieved to see him run off to join his friends (relieved and still momentarily dazzled: *He has friends!*).

He asks Barb if it isn't awkward, having the school nearby now, but she laughs. "They're good neighbors, actually. Private school; crunchy, liberal parents." She gives him a look. "Best of all, the antis don't like the little ones to see them yelling or waving bloody signs. Plus, the one time they trespassed on school grounds, the principal told them off."

He can believe it. He's seen her freeze a dozen kids with a frown.

The only protester in evidence is standing vigil at the end of the drive beside an eight-foot-tall cross.

"Impressive."

"Oh, Ross. I'll tell you his secret. He has a little caster fixed to the foot of it, wheels it away at the end of the day like a golf bag. We call him 'Holy Roller.'

"How are you?" she asks.

"Good. Better."

She beams.

"And you?"

"Outstanding!" She's training to be a doula.

He must look startled. As if Barb were looking for her own absolution.

"Yeah. Doc got me into it. You know she splits her days between the clinic and the hospital?"

(He hadn't.) "Doing . . . deliveries?"

"Sure. Don't look so confused. It's called 'pro-*choice*' for a reason, you know. Supporting women who choose to have kids *and* those who don't."

"Of course," he agrees hastily, but silently he exults, *Both! Both! Both!*

Behind her a car pulls slowly into the lot, the anti stands a little straighter.

"Gotta go." Her smile crooks. "We all have our Ross to bear."

It's a small town, after all. Comes a moment when he recognizes a face, he doesn't know where from. They're at a store, he and the boy. Or maybe a café, the movies. A woman. They smile hesitantly, exchanges pleasantries, he waves her ahead in line—the kind of gesture he likes to make in front of the child to set a good example. She thanks him, beams at the boy, asks his name, and in that moment he recognizes her, recalls the context of their last encounter, even her Barb-bestowed nickname—"Scary Poppins," on account of her black umbrella—and his face must change, betray him. She sees it, though her puzzlement tells him she hasn't placed him yet. Instead, she reads his flinch as a rejection, as if he's smelled something bad, spotted spinach in her teeth, guessed her age. And then slowly it comes to her too. They stare at each other over the boy's head, and the father feels himself tense—to what? Cover her mouth? Cover his son's ears? But she only gives the barest of nods, turns away. A small mercy, a narrow escape.

What are the odds?

"Who was that?" the boy asks.

"Just someone."

It's a small town after all. Eventually you're bound to run into someone who thinks you're a baby killer.

He never recognizes a client from the clinic, but those women he only saw once. Still, it makes him wonder how long he'd have volunteered before someone he knew came along. A friend, a neighbor. A student.

Another reason he's relieved he quit.

He doesn't like to know too much about his students, get too close. Not that he doesn't like them, often he does, but something he insists on in class is that they must treat each other's work as fiction, avoid the autobiographical assumption. Comments like "I'm *so* sorry that happened to you" are out of bounds, as inadmissible as the writer's limp defense "It's all true." *It doesn't matter!* he tells them. The truth isn't always credible; sometimes it's downright inconceivable. ("In-con-*ceiv*able!" as he hears it from *The Princess Bride*, the boy's old favorite.)

Lately, though, a couple of his students have babysat the boy. He watches them read to him—now who's *in loco parentis?*—feels bizarrely like a grandfather. The same feeling he gets when he meets the boy's teachers, and they're all younger than him.

There's an equation they never talk about. Technically, an inequality.

(The father is the one who does math with the boy—they used to do LEGO at the dinner table; now they do math—for which he earns the nickname "the Ruiner," for ruining the boy's fun. A supervillain's name! The father is hurt, tries to make a joke of it, get the boy to give the mother one. "The Amomination?" he suggests hopefully, but it doesn't stick.)

Would they have had the boy if they had had the girl first? A question in two parts:

1. *Would they have had the boy if they had had a healthy girl?*

Probably not, the father thinks. He's an only child himself. They started late. He's not sure they could have afforded a second. Besides, as they tell each other, just about their only parenting "skill" is outnumbering the child.

2. *Would they have had the boy if they hadn't had the abortion?*

Technically, the outcome of one coin flip doesn't depend on another. But what if it determines whether you'll even flip again?

Does this make it more or less likely that they'll ever tell the boy? the father wonders. The secret hangs over them, dark and massive as an asteroid. It makes them bow their heads.

Amomination, he whispers in the darkness. *Ruiner,* she replies.

They used to call each other "Baby," "Babe." He doesn't remember when they stopped, who stopped first. We thought we were being ironic, she notes. Now it seems weirdly sincere. We *were* babies. Such babies!

One nickname that does catch on. Among themselves, giggling and shushing, they call the hypochondriacal grandmother "the Gram Reaper." They laugh like hyenas. They laugh like drains. Guilty, dirty laughter. The best kind. A bad laugh even better than a good cry.

Deep, dark parental secrets, as typically revealed in stories (a partial list):

A Lie Someone Told You About Yourself

We're getting a divorce!

We're *not* your parents!

I ... am your father! We bought you/sold you/left you/found you.* You have a half-/twin/mad/evil brother/sister!* (*Delete as appropriate.) Never: We deleted your sister.

The time comes when they can feel almost nostalgic for the boy's childhood, the phases that pass so swiftly. He will never be four again, never be five again, never be six again. Another birthday, and another, and another. The longest day. The longest day. The longest day.

The first time the boy sleeps over at a friend's, they wander the house as if they've lost something. Not him, but their old selves.

Later on his first over-night school trip—Chicago!—they'll go to dinner and a movie, get drunk, dance, make noisy love. And still, in the spinning darkness afterward, the house will feel hollow and they, bereaved.

"It's not like it was before him," she'll whisper. "It's what it'll be like after."

In the garden, a stepping stone the boy made, a bird feeder.

On the fridge, a collage. On the mantel, a card. On the sill, a crooked vase.

The smudge of a sticker peeled off a door, the chip in a bowl, scratches on the wood floor. He's everywhere and nowhere.

An older friend warns: "It goes even faster when they get to ten, eleven, twelve. The worst is their teens. You're missing their childhood, but really you're mourning your own youth."

Every summer now: a clear-out of old clothes and toys and books the boy has outgrown. It has to be done, the mother and father tell each other. They wade into closets, sort through storage bins, linger over tiny T-shirts, past treasures. The boy who loved them so fiercely for an hour or a week, who slept with them, bathed with them, begged for them, named them, has no sentiment about these things. It's the mother and father who find it hard to let them go. When the father finally takes a couple of boxes to a musty resale store—*Buy Buy Baby*—he's offended at how little he gets, feels cheap for selling these memories. There are other secondhand stores—*Klassic Kids, Boomerang!*—but from then on they donate everything to Goodwill, Kiwanis, the Salvation Army. As if it all belonged to someone we've lost, he can't help thinking, handing them over to a blowzy volunteer, and in a way he guesses they have. First the baby, then the toddler, the preschooler, the kindergartener, gone forever.

Perhaps this is why parents have another, the father thinks.

An heir and a spare.

Someone to hand down the hand-me-downs to.

But it's too late for them, and in truth it feels like tempting fate. It occurs to him, *Could we make the same decision twice, now on the other side of having a child?* Yes, he thinks, but also, if it was hard before, how much, how infinitely harder after having a child?

Instead, it's another summer, another clear-out. It reminds him of that famous short story, he tells her. The shortest in the world so-called. Often (though probably apocryphally) attributed to Hemingway. "For Sale: baby shoes, never worn." *More* tragic subtext! What is it with this guy? "But what if the baby were just too big for them," she says. "Or grew too fast," he says. "Or just *hated* wearing shoes?" "Or friends—no, no, *grandparents!*—bought him ugly-ass ones?"

"And they called him Papa!"

What the father knows is if we lost our child, I'd never sell those shoes.

That's what they should call those resale places, he thinks: *Lost Generation.*

They only actually lost the boy once, not counting a few panicky seconds in stores when he trundled down a different aisle. They were in a hotel, the father had turned to say something to the mother, and when they turned back the boy was in the elevator, the doors closing like jaws. They'd stood there stunned, not as if he'd vanished, but as if he'd never existed, and then—*Stairs? Wait here!*—the father pounding to the next floor and the next and the next until the silver box slid open and the boy yelled, *Peekaboo!*

A couple from their prenatal class are expecting again. A cousin and her husband, too. Parents at pickup. They all know what to expect now—"economies of scale!" one dad jokes—but their children don't. One little girl parrots what she's been told in a conspiratorial whisper. "There's a baby in my mommy's tummy."

"A baby what?" he teases. "A baby mouse? A baby rabbit?"

"No, silly! A baby brother or a baby sister!"

A brother or a sister, he thinks, that old coin toss, but definitely a baby.

It's no different in kind to what he and his wife have said to the boy. *You lived in Mom's belly for nine months.* It's just how people talk, he knows. Baby talk about babies. Better than the old bullshit about storks or gooseberry bushes. Better than going into clinical detail.

Only there's no comparable formula, no script, for telling children about lost siblings. Or maybe there is for miscarriages, he doesn't know mercifully. There certainly isn't one for abortions.

There's no need, he supposes. An abortion can be kept secret, after all. It's not an arrival, but a departure. Except, where's the line between a secret—between privacy and discretion—and shame.

"Will I have a brother or a sister?" the boy asked once. "Would you like one?" the father asked carefully. "God, no!" the mother said. *"Phew!"* They all laughed, profoundly relieved.

The father remembers yearning for a sibling when he was a kid. Only children were rare then, in life and in all the books he read where siblings—Dick, Jane—were the norm. When he asked his mother recently why they'd only had him, she told him she had planned on a large family, but he was such a difficult baby, he put her off having more. *Now you tell us!* his wife lamented, laughing. But lying awake he thinks, now, of those other babies, his unborn siblings, unborn because of him—his fretting, his wailing, his sleep-lessness—searches himself for guilt, as if rooting through pockets for change. Comes up with only lint.

Unborn thanks to birth control, he assumes. He couldn't ask his mother, even now, if she had an abortion, but assumes she would have told them before now if she had. Except if she'd had one, while he was a kid, it would have still been illegal just.

Of course, you wouldn't tell a kid about an abortion, the father knows, any more than any parent would share count-less mysteries of grown-up life. But even when he thinks about telling a *grown* child, he still feels a hesitation. A hesitation born of shame, or more truthfully of fear, fear of judgment, which is perhaps what shame amounts to.

And the most frightening judgment in the world—the last judgment, in a sense, the one that outlives us—is our child's. And still we—even us, he thinks—routinely tell children, *There's a baby in there!*

Just a children's story—simple and innocent. A story that might be true or only make believe. But one, if told often enough, that sticks. *A baby! In there! Just like you!* One that becomes childish when believed by the adults who tell it; believed by the adults our children grow up to be. Such innocence in adults seems suddenly grotesque to him. Big babies! He pictures the giant sculptures of infants by Ron Mueck he saw once: all cuteness rendered monstrous at large scale.

The problem, he knows, is imagination. His old friend, his stock in trade. Imagination is what makes an embryo a baby, a fetus a child. We imagine the future. But, like everything else, there are two sides to imagination. Our hopes *and* our fears. But who wants to face the fears when we're talking about a pregnancy. Only those who have to, he thinks bleakly. Otherwise, our very existence—we were all born after all!— biases us toward hope.

So it's a baby in there. As if saying so will make it so.

Among the many synonyms he knows for *imagine*—to think, dream up, make up, devise, invent, create: to conceive.

*   *   *

In writing classes, he often advises his students to delete extra siblings. Do you *really* need them? Do they add to the story, or dilute it? If they don't have a name, or any dialogue . . . He sticks out his tongue, crosses his eyes, draws a thumb across his neck. And everyone laughs.

When people used to ask him, after his first book came out, which was his favorite story, he used to demur, say it was like asking someone who their favorite kid was, this before he was even a parent. At least, he thinks now, that's one choice he doesn't have to make.

But then, of course, it comes to him, a belated shiver:

We did have another.

Pregnancy, he recalls his wife complaining, is so fucking public. Literally making your fucking public, its consequence at least. People, strangers, feel free to comment on your body, to ask when you're due, to touch your belly. She hated that, the invasion of privacy, the presumptuousness, the taint of the salacious. And babies are public—everyone craning to see into strollers, offering congratulations, parenting tips. Feeding them, changing them, getting mad at them—all often public. It's mostly well meaning, he tried to tell her. Until it isn't, she said, until it spills into people feeling like they have a stake in your pregnancy, your baby, a right to an opinion, a judgment. They know one thing about you, and they think it's everything.

The only people who like it, in her view, are the celebrity

moms. They get to pretend they're normal and *still* get all the attention. She loathes the way they make it look so easy. You know they all have live-in nannies. Baby wranglers, he nods. Stunt moms, daddy doubles, prop babies! And then they all get to write kids' books!

Celebrity abortions not so much, she notes dryly.

Babies in fiction tend to be props, is something he's also told classes. More objects than characters until they can talk. Never quite fully alive on the page.

(As it happens, his proposed summer school class is on fiction by celebrities. *Franco, Ringwald, Hawke, Fisher, Penn, Duchovny, Hanks.* The new classics! They need the money; he needs to make sure the class will fill.)

Each spring, when the studio photographer comes to school to take portraits of the kids, she comes with baby animals for the kids to pose with. One year its chicks, another rabbits. The boy cradles them, beaming.

A baby rabbit, they read together in some children's book, is called a kit.

A baby mouse is called a pinkie.

A baby in the womb, he tells himself firmly, is called a zygote. Or an embryo. Or a fetus.

But can you tell a child that? Better to say it's a "maybe" in there. Or maybe the old bullshit—parsley beds, cabbage patches, watermelon seeds!—was best after all. Stories like Santa and the Easter Bunny that we grow out of.

Gooseberry bush and parsley bed, he googles, were nineteenth-century slang for pubic hair.

The stork myth likely derives from their migration and return nine months later. It was popularized by Hans Christian Andersen. Except in Andersen's story, to punish children who have taunted them, the storks deliver dead babies.

As for the old line about getting pregnant from swallowing watermelon seeds, it reminds him of an older female friend who once described giving birth as like "shitting a watermelon, studded with razor blades."

Very soon now it'll be the Age of Games—*The Hunger Games, Ender's Game*—all the young-adult apocalypses. "YApocalypse Now," the father calls the genre, a favorite of his undergrads too. (*Not literature,* he tells them. *Won't last. Who's going to want to read it after the actual apocalypse!* But, of course, they don't believe in posterity, even though they *are* posterity. When they ask him what he writes, he tells them: *Pre-apocalyptic fiction.*)

In every one of these futures, children are tested, over and over. And in these stories, parents *and* children die. That's really why he can't stand them. He hasn't been able to read books or watch movies with child-in-peril plots since he became a father. He knows he'd die for his child if it came to that—willingly, eagerly—because how to go on living without your child?

No wonder we're so protective, he thinks. Our *own* lives

are at stake. It's our blood in that brimful cup. No, you couldn't go on without your child.

Unless you have another, in which case you have to.

But the closest he's come to protecting his child from death was carrying him to the basement during a tornado warning. They built LEGOs together while winds tore overhead and the sky turned jade.

The mother's pet peeve, by contrast, is all those impossibly perfect TV babies. The ones who sleep through fistfights, rough sex, lengthy exposition. The ones who never cry when the bad guys are closing in—*Oh please! They'd be so dead in real life!*

Terrorists, hitmen, zombies. He'd readily die at their hands for his child. And kill for him, too? He thinks so.

For instance, that story, that line—"I'm cunting"—that's not quite how it happened.

In reality, the father had been asked to pick a favorite word in reply to some writers' thread. He'd gone for "fountain" because, as he explained, the boy had just pointed out a tree in leaf, said it was "like a fountain." His first simile!

Someone had tweeted back: *Another smug parent. Reminds me of my favorite word—cunt.* Some British guy—they use the word more loosely there, often in reference to other men.

(An awkward bit of contextualization—what his students call an "info dump," though they'd probably be relieved to know he didn't use the word about a woman as in the earlier version.)

"The guy's calling me a cunt!" he'd raged, to his wife, in front of their child, until she shushed him. He'd taken her advice, not replied, but he'd looked the guy up, tracked him down, found his address, fantasized about what he'd do if he ever went there. He was offended, of course, but also something worse, something primitive. As if it wasn't just him who'd been insulted, but somehow the boy attacked. Only fantasies, of course—however bloody (*'I'll cunt you, motherfucker!'*)—but then it *was* only a tweet. What might he do in real life?

And this guy only called him a name.

It's the same rage he felt at the clinic. Or related to it. Brother to it. Sister.

"Everyone's a critic," his wife reminded him. "Everyone's a critic of everything."

And this is also what the internet is for, he thinks. If online porn universalizes shame, social media universalizes judgment. Both exercises in self-gratification.

(On the other hand, maybe it was being called "smug," when he feels so abject as a parent, that really set him off.)

* * *

And then there's another school shooting. They're numbingly frequent, but this is the first since the boy started school. And the father feels powerless. What if you can't die, or kill, to protect your child? What if you're not that lucky?

The school principal emails tips for how to talk to a child about bad news. They sit the boy down. They're nervous, but he's calm. They have lockdown drills at school, he explains patiently, he knows what to do.

They didn't know about the drills (they don't read all the principal's emails). They're relieved, and appalled. But the boy is calm, matter-of-fact. He is reassuring *them*. As if it were all perfectly normal, mundane as a fire drill, sensible as looking both ways before you cross or not talking to strangers.

The father is not calm. He rages at the politicians sending their thoughts and prayers. (Here's a thought: Did your prayers get answered last time?) Rages at the NRA flacks talking about the Constitution (Rights! What about wrongs? Let's talk about wrongs for once.)

It's the shamelessness that incenses him.

He fantasizes about protesting a gun store. Standing outside with his own bloody placard showing gunshot fatalities, the number of gun deaths. Shouting "Baby killers" at customers, coming and going. Demanding a waiting period for gun purchases as long as for abortions. Demanding that gun buyers look at photos of gunshot wounds before purchase. Flinging spray patterns of fake blood on the walls of the store.

Enough! his wife tells him. How're you any better than them with all these bullshit fantasies of killing and dying. For our child! Your job is to *live* for him. Isn't that hard enough?

He nods, chagrined. Though secretly he remains certain that in the event of the cabin losing pressure, when oxygen masks drop from a panel above, he'll secure the boy's first, before his own.

When they were growing up, he and his wife, their parents told them not to waste food. Shamed them.

Don't you know there are starving children in India/ Africa/ China? As if cleaning your plate would help them.

Now, they teach the boy to recycle, to compost, not to waste paper, not to waste water. *Or there won't be enough when you're older.* As if the end of the world were his fault, when what they mean is that they won't be there to save him from it. Another shame, generational this time.

All those kids' books about dinosaurs, it comes to him now, are *past*-apocalyptic fiction. All those plastic raptors, all those plush tyrannosaurs. Barney! *C'mon, kids, let's go see fossils in the museum! On the way, we can burn some in the car! Stu-pendous!*

"We used to want things to be better for our kids," his wife whispers. "Now we raise them on mass extinction."

His own father, the boy's grandfather, begins to fail. His memory is going and then his body, as if he's forgotten his body, how to make it work. He clutches seatbacks for balance, shudders tables and shelves. On family visits the father watches the grandmother bend down and tap each of the grandfather's feet one after another to remind him which one to move when he walks. He sees the grandfather freeze in perplexity before his armchair, unsure of how to turn, arrange his limbs, lower himself into it.

There are tests (the grandmother resists them). There are exercises (the grandfather forgets to do them). There is equipment (canes and walkers, white plastic grab-handles for the bathroom). There are doctors and nurses and physical therapists and helpers (to cherish and complain about). There are hospitals and facilities and homes (to tour and put their names down for).

"Second childhood," the grandmother calls it. She hasn't slept through the night in a year.

Sometimes he takes the boy on these visits. Later he doesn't. He promises the grandmother he'll bring her grandson again when the grandfather is in a home. He uses this as leverage.

The grandfather is no good with babies, never once held the boy as a baby. It made the father think about their relationship, when he was a boy and the grandfather was a new father. But the grandfather is better with toddlers—playful, teasing. *Got your nose!* On a visit before his body begins to betray him, he cuts a small, neat hole in the lawn with a trowel for the boy to golf. He rummages in the attic for bald tennis balls, fraying shuttlecocks, deflated soccer balls. Treasures to the boy, relics of his own childhood to the father. In the evenings the grandfather gets impatient, snappish, but afternoons in the garden, the two fathers watch the boy together.

"You have kids?" the grandfather asks once, companionably. By now the father has learned not to contradict him when he's confused. He plays the part as required—old army buddy, office mate, school chum—mostly by nodding and listening and prompting.

"No," he says now. "Would you recommend it?"

"Oh, yes! Life's empty without them. My advice, find a nice girl, start a family before you get too long in the tooth."

Later, in the home, the grandfather will look at the boy and call him by the father's name, ask him if he's been good, share candy with him. But the grandfather will only look at the father, his own son, and frown. As if he doesn't know him or, worse, as if he knows he's the one who put him here. For the father, watching grandson and grandfather together is like looking at an old family photo. He can see the love, but he can't quite feel it.

At least the boy enjoys visiting Grandpa. The caregivers dote on him. He begs for rides on Grandpa's lap in his wheelchair. Afterward, the pair of them sit happily together watching the fish in the aquarium, gliding back and forth, back and forth, while the father talks to the nurses.

The boy is fearless. Snakes and spiders at the zoo fascinate him. Jellyfish on the beach. He runs to see the Madagascar hissing cockroach as if it were an old friend. At the Sears Tower he bounces and sprawls on the glass floor of the viewing platform, the city yawning beneath him.

The boy is terrified. Of bees, of shots, of curly slides (he split his lip on one once). The threats he knows, can imagine. Of death he has no sense. The father wonders when that will come, what it'll mean. Lost toys, broken toys, floating goldfish—these are the tiny harbingers.

And then the hamster dies. "She was old and in pain," the father explains. "The vet put her down." *Down where?* "Put her to sleep, I mean." *When will she wake up?* "They're euphemisms," the father explains. *White lies?* "Kind lies." The boy nods.

The real lie, the bit he leaves out, is that he had a choice. The vet put her down, true, but first she asked him what he wanted to do. A formality. The animal was in pain, on its side, legs turning stiffly, no hope and nothing to do. But still, "I have to ask." He had paused, frozen really, and the vet frowned in her white coat, explained it all again as if to an idiot. No hope. Painless. Quick. A mercy. And *still* he'd been unable to say. She told him she'd give them a moment alone. *Them*—him and the hamster. Though he suspected it was only an excuse for her to step away before she lost her patience. He felt like a fool. He feared telling the child. He thought about lying. He thought about asking for a second opinion. He thought about calling his wife. Instead, he thanked the hamster, "for being a good pet." Oh, he felt like a fool. Apologized to the hamster, anyway. Stroked its shivering side. Told it, "Goodbye, girl." *Jesus!* He was sweating, shaking when the vet came back, but he managed to nod, to stay for the end.

At home they find a small box, dig a small hole, have a small funeral. "We put her down *in the ground*," the boy tells his mother with solemn precision. Their son believes in Santa, the Easter Bunny, the Tooth Fairy, the Force, and now heaven. But that night he asks shyly, "Can we get a cat now?"

And the father—stricken with grief, stricken with embarrassment at his own grief—promises, chokingly, "Sure!"

When the boy was a baby, they took turns to put him down, to put him to sleep.

"Thanks for taking care of that," the mother says that night, and he shrugs. *Taking care*, he thinks. *Is that what it was?* What he says is: "No need for us both to be there."

Some parents have funerals for their aborted fetuses, he has heard. Their genetic counselor had suggested a similar ceremony of remembrance. *It eases some people. We have a quiet place if you'd like to use it.* But they shook their heads. How do you mourn something you killed?

Now there's talk of some states mandating such funerals.

If only a mercy killing included some mercy for the killers.

He suddenly remembers friends, a couple, years ago who when they knew they were having a baby got rid of their cat. They'd heard that cats can smother infants, attracted by the smell of milk on their breath. An urban legend—he checks—a superstition dating back to the sixteen and seventeenth centuries, likely influenced by the idea of cats as witches' familiars. What he can't recall is how the couple got rid of the cat. Whether they killed it or gave it away or abandoned it. Whether the cat was alive or dead. Will a vet even put a healthy cat to sleep? he wonders. The answer, yes; the term of art, "convenience euthanasia."

He finds that shocking for a split second.

In any event, it turns out they *can't* get a cat now. Turns out the boy is allergic; he comes home from a friend's house with itchy eyes. Allergic and inconsolable. For days, he mourns the cat he never had.

The father is secretly relieved. An older colleague told him once cats were baby substitutes. "They weigh the same, they sleep on you, they roll around on their backs kicking their legs in the air. They mewl." "What about dogs?" he asked the same animal lover. "Kids! 'Tweens and teens, tearing around in circles in the park, chasing each other, rolling in the mud, yapping."

And smaller creatures? he doesn't ask. Mice, gerbils, hamsters? Fish?

At the zoo, the father recalls, everyone's favorites are the monkeys, the meerkats, the lemurs. The animals that *play*. The rest—listless or neurotic—are inmates, lifers, imprisoned and institutionalized. Adults, in other words. A tiger rips at a cardboard box, the kind refrigerators come in, shredding it with long, lazy twists of his huge head. Doing the recycling, the father thinks with a nod of recognition to the big cat.

* * *

The boy settles for Snoopy. *Peanuts* is his new favorite. They hear him chuckling manically from under the covers after lights-out. He's taken to exclaiming *Good grief!* at every opportunity.

Clean your plate. *Good grief!*

Tidy your room. *Good grief!*

What do you say? *Good grief!*

But why, the father wonders, did Schrödinger pick a cat? It's a thought experiment—he could have put anything in the box. A mouse, a rat, a rabbit—those traditional experimental subjects. Why not a dog or a monkey or an elephant, for that matter (it's a thought experiment—no apparatus to build, the box could be as big as a house)? Did Schrödinger *have* a cat? Have something against cats? The father imagines a mouse in a box—wouldn't it make noise, rustle around? You'd know it's status without looking. But a cat, a cat could just sleep in there. (And in fact, more recent versions of the thought experiment imagine not poison, but knockout gas in the box, so that the cat might be either awake or asleep. But really, how sentimental are we that we need to imagine a humane *thought* experiment? We can imagine a quantum paradox, but not the death of a cat.)

Schrödinger is said to have owned a cat called Milton. Or Toby. To-by or not To-by, as the joke goes. Its existence is likely apocryphal.

It is known he had a dog. And an aunt who owned six cats, whose "yowling" (the cats' not the aunt's) he disapproved.

He disapproved of his own cat, too, of course, called his famous paradox a "ridiculous case," intended it as a critique of quantum theory, its "blurred model" of reality. "There is a difference between a shaky or out-of-focus photograph and a snapshot of clouds and fog banks." Or, as Einstein wrote in agreement: "One cannot get around the assumption of reality—if only one is honest." Both of them loath to believe that atomic randomness could give rise to real-world uncertainty.

If only, the father thinks.

Winters they go to the botanical gardens to bask in the hothouse fug; to the park with the good sledding hill; to the mall to see Santa in his fat suit; to the local petting farm to see Jesus in his manger, live goats and sheep and chickens and cows grazing among the plaster figures.

Does it start here, the father thinks, or at the art museum, another winter destination, with all those Madonna-and-childs lining the walls as if the Renaissance were one big Mommy and Me class. Is this where the deification of babies begins?

"Not forgetting the impossible standard set by Mary," his wife points out. "Mother *and* virgin. No competing with that." She stands before a beatific painting of the holy family. "Talk about smug parents." The father nods. He's lousy at DIY, stumped by IKEA instructions, can't even live up to Joseph. "And to think," the wife whispers, moving on, "underage girl, pregnant by someone other than her husband, she'd be a prime candidate ..."

The boy comes home from school with colds; he comes home with coughs. He gives them to his parents, face flushed and shining, as if presenting a painting he's actually proud of. But how not to kiss a sick child, how not to hug him, as if love will cure him. When in fact he cures himself, invariably within twenty-four to forty-eight hours, while his parents catch cold for a week, marveling at his immune system—envious and reassured.

Only when he comes home with lice does his mother scream, "Stay away from me!"

He comes home with valentines and black eyes. He comes home with homework and paperwork. The only thing he doesn't come home with are both gloves.

They enroll him in soccer. He loves watching it on TV, and the view is even better from the field as he stands and watches the other kids run around him.

They enroll him in ballet. It's good for balance and coordination, but at the recital he freezes, until coaxed off the stage into the father's arms. The boy sits on his lap for the rest of the show, the pair of them performing their love.

Swim club, flag football, street hockey, basketball come and go with the seasons. Then it's soccer again. And the boy scores a goal! And the father thinks his heart will burst.

At college all his students are writing coming-of-age stories. It's the Age of Coming of Age.

When he first started teaching, he worried he was too young, only a few years ahead of many of them. He used to dress up—*dress to profess,* his wife called it—in jacket and tie. It took him a while to figure out that teaching, simply standing up in front of a board, adds ten years.

Back then being *in loco parentis* felt like a fraud; now the students look like children. He used to hope they'd keep him young; now they make him feel mortal.

They keep on coming of age, he groans, class after class, year after year. It's exhausting.

You'd be out of work otherwise, his wife points out.

It's true. His livelihood depends on procreation. There are students not yet conceived that he'll teach before he retires.

And you need the job, she reminds him, nodding at the boy, to pay for his college.

"What do you want to be when you grow up?"

"A soccer player," the boy says. His backup plan is astronaut.

The father wanted to be a crossing guard at that age. "Lollipop Ladies," he called them, for the stop signs they carried.

"Why?"

He can't remember. Maybe to look after people.

And then he wanted to be a writer.

"And now you are one!"

The father isn't sure this is a good lesson. You can be anything you want to be, except the boy isn't going to be a professional soccer player. Yet secretly he thinks this is the great achievement of his life, the source of his happiness, that he grew up to be what he'd always wanted to be. *Almost* always wanted.

A crossing guard! But somehow escorting kids across a busy street, staring down the traffic with nothing but a sign (a cross between a lance and a shield), was the closest thing to heroism in his young life. He still feels a righteous rage when cars roll through the intersection in front of their house.

Of course, he's also grown up to be a man who aborts babies, puts his own father in a home.

His mother asked him once—no, she didn't *ask*, didn't dare, instead she *told* him—how hard that must have been for him, and he nodded heavily. But it wasn't. Not really. Not *compared*. It wasn't a choice; it was an eventuality. Besides it's not like he was killing his father. Something else—time, age, Alzheimer's—will take care of that, only infinitely more slowly. And who is that a mercy for?

His father had told him once, years earlier, half in jest, half in earnest, if he ever *got like that*—they were talking about his grandmother, far gone by then—*just do me in, knock me on the head.* But the day hasn't yet come when old people are put to sleep like animals.

Yet.

He wonders what his own son will do when he grows up. What he is teaching him.

t is the Age of *Doctor Who*. Time travel. That perennial fantasy. They read H. G. Wells together. The father can't wait to show him *Terminator, Star Trek, Back to the Future*. The DVD player, a time machine to take them back to his own nerdy youth.

They read *A Wrinkle in Time*.

"What would you do if you had a time machine?" he asks the boy. "Grow up!" "Your little body already *is* a time machine." "Grow up faster." (He yearns to be THIS tall to ride.) "What would *you* do?" the boy asks.

"Travel to the future to see you all grown up."

"Silly, you'll be there already."

"But older!"

"Oh, right." He ponders this gravely. "Too old to play, like Grandpa."

"But my younger self could."

The boy nods against his chest.

And the past? the father wonders, after the boy's light is out. What would he change? What would he undo? When would he go back to?

That day the boy fell downstairs, he thinks. To catch him as he tipped.

But that last's a lie. The boy did fall downstairs that one time, but it's not the moment the father would go back to. That was a little later, the boy on the potty, crying, trying to get up, the father holding him down with one hand. But the circumstances don't matter. The father had slapped the boy. Not hard, but that doesn't matter either. Just to get his attention, to snap him out of it. But none of it matters. It was the instinctiveness, the absence of thought, the hand flicking out. A reflex. If he could go back, he'd stop it. Protect the boy from himself.

Another time he snapped at the boy, *You never think of anyone else,* and the boy, red-faced, told him, *Yes, I do! I love you more than anything in the world.* A tantrum of love. A memory the father cherishes, though he cringes at the thought of the anger that provoked it.

The past.

One winter afternoon, a deer trotting up their residential street. *Look, look!* A scatter of hoofbeats. And then it vaults the neighbor's fence.

A fall morning, on their way to see the marching band before the game, walking through the student ghetto, an armchair on fire in the middle of a yard.

That spring, a backhoe in their driveway—Mike Mulligan!—demolishing the old garage, glass raining, rotten splinters somersaulting through the air.

All of it perfectly normal to the boy; so much so that all he can say of the deer is "It should be on the sidewalk!" like someone's dog; so much so, he'll shake his head in years to come when one or the other says, *Remember when?* and he replies, *Oh, you mean the past.* The mercy and horror being that he won't remember *any* of this.

But do we? she asks him. He knows what she means. Those years are already becoming hazy, each age erasing the last. Vivid moments emerge out of a white mist. He puts it down to sleep deprivation. The past feels less remembered than dismembered.

The look of shy wonder on the boy's face in the rearview, driving home from the pet store, a cardboard box in his lap, a hamster, rustling inside.

The same look as you, the mother says, when you first held him in the hospital.

The father is *almost* completely certain the boy doesn't remember that slap.

But, of course, he can't ask.

* * *

And the future.

In the future his own father will die. The boy may barely remember him, and if at all only in his twilight state. What will he tell the boy about his grandfather? What stories?

The father is a writer, after all. His first published story, in fact, was about his grandmother, his father's mother, her own struggles with dementia. His father didn't altogether like it, his writing about her, about the family. Luckily, the writer used to think, though perhaps also by choice, his father wasn't a reader, didn't read his son's work. Had he, he might have thought it a betrayal of sorts, disrespectful. Parents keep secrets from children; children are not supposed to reveal their parents' secrets.

The grandmother he wrote about is long dead now; the writer's father himself barely remembers her. Very soon now his story will be all that's left of her.

He doesn't feel guilty, the writer, for writing about his grandmother, or about his parents as he has also done. Who else will tell a parent's story if not a child, after all? How else will they be remembered? To him it seems the natural order of things. Writers write against death, it is said, for posterity, for immortality. But not necessarily, or primarily, their own.

Telling a story about a child, though? Telling a version of a life that is still soft, still forming? Like a fontanel.

In his writing classes the father talks about appropriation, the taking and telling of other people's stories. Young writers get exercised about these things, what they are and aren't allowed to write. They just want to be good people, he knows, except he's not sure writers *are* good people (or even should be; maybe it helps to write flawed human characters, if you are one). Certainly they're no respecters of rules. All fiction is appropriation. Only the narrowest, most solipsistic memoir— of life on a desert island, say—doesn't appropriate from others. Still some appropriations, he knows, are more charged than others. It's a challenge for a woman to write a male character, but it's a different challenge for a man to write a female character (and yes, for a man to write about abortion). For a Black writer to write a white character is one thing; for a white writer to write a Black character something else again. Something shaped by society, and history, by power and the abuse of power. Writers are no respecters of rules, of "don't" or "can't," but he wants his students to understand them in order to break them. To be good writers, if not good people.

Yet isn't the ultimate power imbalance between parents and children? For a child to write about a parent is one thing; for a parent to write about a child something else. And he still wants to be a good parent.

But what if this is not *about* his son, the father tells himself, but *for* his son?

Sometimes his students ask him who he writes for, who his ideal reader is, and it came to him recently—his best reader is his wife; his *ideal* reader is his son, though he can barely read yet, and certainly not the kind of things he writes . . . but one day.

He used to think he wrote for immortality. Once he had his son, he worried he'd lose that desire, that procreation was the more essential hedge against mortality. Maybe so, but now it occurs to him his son is the physical embodiment of posterity. The posterity whose judgment he yearns for. And cowers from.

This is how you tell him, he tells himself. *How you tell him you love him. How you tell him you killed his sister. How you tell him he wouldn't be here if you hadn't.* Because she couldn't be his "sister"; they couldn't be "siblings." They were alternatives, two sides of the same coin, both heads, but always and forever facing away.

And how you wouldn't have it any other way. He is the child of abortion and the end of regret.

We had an abortion and then we had a child. But also: we had a child and then we had an abortion. The koan of their lives.

A writer he knows suggests it's superstition, this reluctance to write about our children. "People don't want to write about their children because they think that, if they do, their children might die." But what if we write about our dead children, he wonders. The darlings we killed?

A writer's job, they say, is to imagine the unimaginable, but he can't imagine life without the boy. Our job, he tells his students instead, is to say the unsay-able, to speak the unspeakable—the unutterable made utterable by virtue of being written, whispered on a page.

But before all that, they *do* get a cat. Hypoallergenic! And not some hairless Dr. Evil model. The breeder sends them fur samples to tuck into their pillowcases, to Band-Aid to their forearms. If they have no reaction, they can have a cat.

They bring her home in the car, the kitten in her crate, the boy alongside, marveling at the trembling, trilling life in the box beside him.

"You have kids, and then they want pets—fish, rodents, pretty soon it's cats and dogs, living together." That same older colleague and friend. "You might have never had pets, or wanted them, but you get 'em anyway, for the kids. And then the kids leave for college and you're left with the pets. You wanted kids and you end up with pets. And you're grateful for the company! Except sometimes, you're not sure if the kids come home because they miss you or the critters."

"But why do we give in and get them the pets?" he wonders.

"Because we love to see them love! Can't get enough of it. I used to think it's because they can never love *us* enough. But that's not it. Their love for pets is a promise that they'll love their own kids. And buy *them* pets! The circle of frigging life . . ."

* * *

The first time the boy goes to sleepaway camp—just a week, just a few hours away—the house feels bigger without him, the days longer. It's as if the space-time continuum has warped. When he Skypes with them, he looks older, as if he's calling from the future.

Without him to animate them, his toys lay strewn about the floor as if across a battlefield, lifeless, soulless. I know how they feel, the father thinks.

The cat stalks from room to room, chirping quizzically, silently shedding.

She's so furry, when she finally settles in a lap, she looks like a hen roosting. But before she lies down, she plumps them like a pillow, working her paws, rhythmically, a behavior said to derive from kittens kneading their mothers before nursing. Perfectly normal, the internet says. Some cats will do this—to men and women alike—all their lives. Suddenly he intuits the comfort of keeping a pet even after the child leaves home.

In a few years, when they nag him to do his chores, his homework, the boy will mock grumble: "Do this, do that, do the cat!" A running joke, one of a series of little repetitive riffs he does—overflows of language, verbal self-stimming. "Wonder where he gets *that* from," the mother will say.

*   *   *

In a few years, the boy who couldn't tie his shoelaces will learn to juggle. The boy who couldn't ride a bike will want to surf. The boy who couldn't climb a jungle gym will scale a climbing wall.

If this *is* a story about him, the father thinks, the boy is its hero—the one who changes.

They used to mark his height against a door frame. Now he stands back to back with his father. Soon he'll be wearing the father's hand-me-downs; in a few years he'll be handing them back.

How do you protect something bigger than yourself? the father asks the mother in bed one night.

He'll ride roller coasters his father refuses to go on. He'll like bands his mother has never heard of.

He'll know things they don't know. Have secrets, and shames, of his own. Shut the bathroom door. Lock the bathroom door. Criticize their driving, their drinking, their swearing. He'll be ashamed of *them*.

They'll be able to go to the bathroom at night without tiptoeing. Go to restaurants that don't serve mac and cheese. Now when they panic that he's quiet-too-quiet, they realize he's just reading, a miracle of stillness, lying on his stomach, just one leg swinging up and down like a metronome.

He'll still need a "bop" sometimes, as he calls it, an arm-flinging, wrist-flapping, kicking up of heels. A caper, a gambol, a rumpus. Leap of faith, and jump for joy. Sometimes they'll even join in, breathless with love.

They finally sort through all those photos.

The boy in costume: at Halloween, but also at pageants and plays, wearing his mom's shoes, his dad's glasses, a cape with his first underpants. (Subsection: funny hats—pilgrim, cowboy, hipster, etc.)

The boy with famous figures: dinosaurs, mascots, waxworks, LEGObama. (Subsection: cute critters—otters, sloths, manatees, etc.)

Taking in the sights: the Lincoln Memorial, the Mall of America, the Magic Kingdom, and the M&M's store.

With food: gawping at birthday cakes and ice cream sundaes big enough to swallow him; wielding Popsicles like light sabers, hot dogs like baseball bats, crab legs like pirate hooks.

And in the background always the same wan extras—her hair still long, *that* dress, *those* glasses, cargo shorts!—so young they look ancient.

In a few more years, he'll travel places they've never been, form opinions they've never held, mention friends they've never met. Fall in—and out—of love with one, move in with another. There might even be a child—a grandchild!—or an abortion, and how will his parents feel then? And what will it matter?

"What if you can't help?" his wife asks him again.

"With any of it." They're out for dinner, the boy at a sleepover. "Oh, you can for a little while, but you can't forever. Can you handle that?"

It's their favorite restaurant, the place they go for occasions—holidays, birthdays, anniversaries. They came when she was pregnant, and when she wasn't. When the boy was in a car seat, a high chair, a booster.

He nods, takes her hand. "Only this is forever." And she rolls her eyes, because of course she does. Because the more the boy changes, the more they stay the same.

The boy will come back to visit, he tells himself. Holidays, birthdays, anniversaries. To look in on us, as he used to look in on his own parents.

The old house, the hometown. The box, he thinks, we're in it now.

The occasion this time is his book, it's finished, coming out soon. She orders a nice bottle. People are going to assume it's all true, she says, that I actually had a drinking problem.

They'll think worse of me, he says.

Maybe. She tops them up. But you deserve it.

She raises her glass; he waits for her toast.

Finally, she grins. Fuck shame, and he nods, clinks. Fuck shame.

*   *   *

But that's not quite right, he thinks later. Toasts aren't true, only what we wish were true, prayers with drinks. Sure, for the longest time he thought shame had fucked them. And of course, sometimes, often, he wishes there were less shame in the world—for the poor, the weak, the othered. Yet other times he wishes there were so much more—that the bankrupt businessmen, the paid-off politicians, the faithless preachers, all the profiteers and hypocrites who fill the news felt it more, felt it at all.

"Shame is the lie someone told you about yourself," according to Anaïs Nin (herself the author of several abortions).

But what if it's not a lie? And what if the someone is you?

It makes him think of Barb, opining one misty morning: "Shame just makes you human. Isn't that the lesson of the Garden? Sure, God creates. But Adam and Eve only become human when they fuck up, when they know shame. And you know who doesn't know shame? The innocent. No shame in the womb." The low winter sun was beginning to break through, casting her shadow in the fog behind her. "You know what the French call us, yeah? *Faiseurs d'anges.* Ooh-la-la! 'Makers of angels.' Better than baby killers, right? But still wrong. We're not making anything; they're *already* angels. Beings of faith. Not yet fallen, not yet human."

Because shame makes us human.

Another thought experiment. Another possibility. Another *what if.*

Barb, herself, of course, isn't human but made-up. A lie someone told you. Named not for Barbara Bush as she claims, but for her series of pointed zingers. For a character trait. Did you wonder? Did you guess? How easy it is to imagine a life.

She might not be real, but she might be right. Maybe shame just means we're alive. *I could have died of shame,* we say, but we don't. *You'll live to regret it,* we say, and we do.

All this talk of shame, he thinks. All these doubts and regrets. And all—miraculously, paradoxically—worth it. Because what comes to him now, when he writes of his son, what he feels most profoundly and purely is pride. The other side of the coin.

They had to explain to the boy what the toy cash register was, but he loved its jangling spring-loaded drawer, filled it with treasures. Susan B. Anthonys, Sacagaweas, JFK half-dollars. Plastic coins, wooden coins, chocolate coins. Replica Roman coins, doubloons, pieces of eight. Ancient Chinese coins with the square holes, heptagonal British change, Mardi Gras favors. Euros, pesos, loonies. Tokens from Chuck E. Cheese.

The Sacagawea dollar is the only coin the father's ever seen with a child on it—a sleeping baby peeking out from the sling on his mother's back. The only way to get two heads with one toss.

The boy would insist on putting coins in slots—vending machines, pinball machines, parking meters.

Once, the car CD player. *Noooo!* He loved coin-operated telescopes at scenic lookouts, those pressed penny machines

175

that for fifty cents flatten a coin, stamp it with a new pattern. In museums, he ran to put coins in donation boxes, could watch them spiral into a gravity well for minutes on end, lazily circling, then racing faster and faster. Ever on edge, never falling, until the final plunge. He'd pour change in until the bowl shrieked and sang with rolling coins, chasing each other like bicycles in the Olympic velodrome.

They always had change—the father's pockets swaying heavily, the mother's purse bulging lumpily—for fountains, for wishes. So many wishes, there was hardly anything left for his piggy bank.

All those coin-spangled fountains and wishing wells. Scooped out after hours by someone in rubber boots. Even now he shies from explaining what happened to all those wishes.

Once, on the walk to school, a flash of copper, like a beacon. The father had paused, caught between the instinct to pick it up and the shame of seeming cheap. A penny isn't much to stoop for, and yet—he heard his father's voice, a child of the war: *They all add up.* And then, as he hesitated, the boy ducked down and snatched it up. "Lucky!" he announced triumphantly, face as shiny as the head on the coin. And the father nodded, smiled, momentarily won over by his conviction.

When did I stop picking up pennies? he wondered. How long has it been? What would they have amounted to?

And, of course, once the boy swallowed a coin. They blame Hanukkah gelt. He claimed he was lying in bed, flip, flip, flipping it, and it just fell in his mouth.

The nurse was reassuring, or as reassuring as anyone can be when saying, *Check his stool.* But they never did find it.

He was wrong about that coin not giving a fuck, the father realizes all these years later. If it did, if it could, it would surely spin forever, hang in the air revolving end over end over end, never, ever fall.

Horsing around one afternoon, he bites his tongue when the boy head-butts him.

His mouth fills with blood.

The taste of pennies is how it's always described in fiction.

But he's never tasted a coin, he realizes. Is this what they taste like? Blood.

Through the window, dusk is descending. The light seems less to fade than to soften and melt into the earth under the weight of shadow. The bare trees are etched, branches like a vast, delicate network of veins, against the pink-tinged sky.

Bedtime! Good night, Sweet Prince! They chase the giggling boy upstairs.

All the years of ritual—undressing and dressing, diaper changes, potty time, bath time, tooth brushing, reading, hugs and kisses—are so *exhausting*. If they don't fall asleep beside him, whoever is on bedtime duty stumbles downstairs, announces wearily, "And that concludes today's parenting." Until the next day, and the next and the next. As if it were a curse and not a blessing. As if it really were forever.

Acknowledgements

It turns out that it also takes a village to publish a novel. Mine includes my "Rock of Agents," Maria Massie; my superteam of editors, Naomi Gibbs, Carole Welch, Helen Atsma, and Lauren Wein; and all the dedicated, talented professionals at Houghton Mifflin Harcourt and Sceptre who backed the book. Sincere thanks to all of them, as well as to my former editors, Jenna Johnson and Janet Silver, for a couple of significant drinks.

The opening section, "Chance," first appeared, in slightly different form, as a short story in *Glimmer Train* back in 2012 and later in *Bob Seger's House and Other Stories, New Stories from the Midwest 2015*, *Catamaran*, and *The Drum*. I'm grateful to the editors of all those publications and to a fellowship from the National Endowment for the Arts, which enabled me to enlarge the original story.

While many books, articles, and sources informed my work, I'm particularly indebted to the insights of Sidonie

Smith, Jane Hassinger, Lisa Harris, and Bernie Klein. The quotation on page 212 is from Anne Enright's *Making Babies*. With respect to the book's material more broadly, a line of Lorrie Moore's seems apt: "This story has a relationship to real life like that of a coin to a head."

Many other thanks are owed, but I'm especially grateful to the following for their kindness along the way: Lisa; Seth and Deb; Joanna, Susan, Shan, Imogen, Sam, Karl, Rachel, Lisa, Josh, and Mary S. and Mary P.; Holly, Rajani, Beth; Daryl, Tim, Lindsay, and Mary Y.; Margaret, Chris, Rachel, Marissa, Christina, and Tricia. I'm forgetting the names of several others, though not their generosity.

Finally, of course, this book would not have been possible without the love and support of my family. Thank you for bearing with me, bearing me up, and simply bearing me.

PETER HO DAVIES

The Fortunes

'A poignant, cascading four-part novel about being
Asian and western, about immigrants and natives, about
belonging in a country and one's skin. It's outstanding.'
David Mitchell, *Guardian*

'Beautifully crafted . . . Though it deals, of necessity, with
racism in all its insidious forms, it does so with humanity,
humour, self-deprecation and a hefty dose of irony'
Mario Reading, *Spectator*

'A prophetic work, with passages of surpassing beauty . . .
a boldly imagined work of fiction in which historic
figures . . . come to an astonishingly vivid, visceral life'
Joyce Carol Oates

The Welsh Girl
Longlisted for the Man Booker Prize

'Moving, memorable and beautifully written . . . a gripping
human story . . . it leaves one thinking about the nature
of cowardice and patriotism, identity and roots'
Jessica Mann, *Sunday Telegraph*

'A beautifully crafted, lyrical novel'
Maggie O'Farrell, *Observer* Books of the Year

'Emotionally resonant and perfectly rendered, I believed in
every character, every sheep, every last blade of grass.'
Ann Patchett

'A scintillating instance of fictional imagination applied to history'
Richard Eder, *New York Times*

SCEPTR